SCOTNOTE
Number 43

GW01458029

The Poetry and Drama of Jackie Kay

Lorna Borrowman Smith

Association for Scottish Literature 2022

Published by
Association for Scottish Literature
Scottish Literature
7 University Gardens
University of Glasgow
Glasgow G12 8QH
www.asls.org.uk

ASL is a registered charity no. SC006535

First published 2022

A CIP catalogue for this title
is available from the British Library

ISBN 978-1-906841-49-2

ASL acknowledges the support of the
Scottish Government towards the publication of this book

**The Scottish
Government**
Riaghaltas na h-Alba

CONTENTS

SCOTNOTES

Study guides to major Scottish writers and literary texts

Produced by the Education Committee
of the Association for Scottish Literature

THE ASSOCIATION FOR SCOTTISH LITERATURE aims to promote the study, teaching and writing of Scottish literature, and to further the study of the languages of Scotland.

To these ends, the ASL publishes works of Scottish literature; literary criticism and in-depth reviews of Scottish books in *Scottish Literary Review*; and scholarly studies of language in *Scottish Language*. It also publishes *New Writing Scotland*, an annual anthology of new poetry, drama and short fiction, in Scots, English and Gaelic. All these publications are available as a single 'package', in return for an annual subscription.

ASL also produces a range of teaching materials covering Scottish language and literature for use in schools.

Enquiries should be sent to:

> ASL
> Scottish Literature
> 7 University Gardens
> University of Glasgow
> Glasgow G12 8QH
>
> Tel/fax +44 (0)141 330 5309
> e-mail **office@asls.org.uk**
> or visit our website at **www.asls.org.uk**

Acknowledgements

I would like to thank the Education Committee of the Association for Scottish Literature for encouraging me to write this study guide. I am most grateful to Ronnie Renton for his editorial guidance and Duncan Jones for his expertise in bringing it to print.

A note on the text

Page references in this *Scotnote* are to the following titles:

Poetry Collections

> *Darling: New & Selected Poems* (Bloodaxe Books Ltd: Northumberland, 2007)
> *Fiere* (Picador: London, 2011)
> *Bantam* (Picador: London, 2017)

Poetic Dramas

> *The Adoption Papers* (contained in *Darling*)
> *The Lamplighter* (Picador: London, 2020)
> (Both of these works are dealt with in this *Scotnote* in their entirety.)

Autobiography

> *Red Dust Road: An Autobiographical Journey* (Picador: London 2017)

1. INTRODUCTION

'You are part fable, part porridge', asserts Jackie Kay in her memoir *Red Dust Road*. This memorable phrase highlights the complex nature of her own and others' identity and can equally be applied to her wide-ranging work in poetry, prose and drama. In much of her work she explores her own life, examining her genetic heritage, her upbringing and the cultural forces which shaped her. Many of her poems illuminate the stuff of everyday life, articulating, often with humour, individuals' experience in its many complexities. She commemorates the love of family and friends in poems of great tenderness and expresses the disappointments of life with a generous spirit devoid of bitterness.

She explores the lives of others, giving marginalised or persecuted individuals, whose identity has been denied to them, a voice. She bears witness to the consequences of the worst in human nature: war, racism and slavery, using dramatic monologue to condemn the blighting and destruction of individual lives.

Through keen observation, historical research and the power of her imagination, Jackie Kay has created a body of work which powerfully reflects the contradictions and complexities of the human condition. In this *Scotnote*, I will discuss the key themes which permeate her work and will highlight the stylistic techniques which she deploys.

In an interview published in the *Scottish Review of Books* 11.3 (2016), Jackie Kay discussed the importance of finding and feeling secure in one's own identity while acknowledging that it is not 'a fixed thing'; that it shifts as a result of many family and cultural influences. She remarks in her memoir that the 'jigsaw' will never be complete. In the same interview she spoke of her need to develop her own voice: 'There has to

1

be a way of capturing your own complexities'. And it is these complexities which she explores in many of her individual poems and her poetic drama *The Adoption Papers.*

Much of her work reflects the stuff, 'the porridge', of everyday life: its joys and celebrations; its disappointments and sorrows. She has stated that poetry should be 'open to everybody' and in her civic role as Makar, Scotland's national poet, she engaged with communities the length and breadth of the country reading her poetry and encouraging the creativity of others. Her attitude to poetry and poetry-making is a democratic one: that it is an essential medium in which to explore personal and communal experience.

Fundamental to her work is the need to give others a voice, particularly 'the voiceless', those who have been marginalised by society or denied their identity by oppressive political and economic forces. Many of her poems express the feelings of women in desperate situations who struggle against all the odds to hold on to their identity. In her poems for children she expresses, often with humour, a child's perception of the world.

In her interview with the *Scottish Review of Books,* Kay stated that: 'I like the voices of people and their syntax and word orders and rhythms and their particular vocabulary'. And it is the uniqueness of individual voices which characterises much of her poetry. Using dramatic monologue rather than traditional verse forms, she structures a narrative in which the speaker expresses his/her own emotional reactions to a particular situation. She uses different language registers in Scots and English; striking imagery; modulations of tone, from strong irony to playful humorous wordplay; and the power of repetition and rhetorical questions to convey the uniqueness of individual lives on the page.

A feature of her writing, found particularly in her poetic drama *The Lamplighter,* is her use of intertextuality, where a quotation or direct reference to another text is embedded in her own work. In *The Lamplighter*, quotations from a slave-ship's log, lines from a parliamentary bill and the personal testimonies of enslaved women are integral to the text. Song is an important feature of her work. Growing up in 'a house of song', Kay was introduced to folk songs, blues, music hall songs and opera. She embeds lines from popular songs, blues and traditional Scots songs in many of her poems and the rhythms and cadences of her poetry have echoes of musical forms.

Jackie Kay was born in Edinburgh in 1961 to a Scottish mother and a Nigerian father. Her birth parents met when her father was a student at the University of Aberdeen and her mother was working as a nurse. She was adopted as a baby by Helen and John Kay and brought up in their home in Bishopbriggs. John Kay worked full time for the Communist Party of Great Britain and Helen Kay was a primary school teacher and the secretary of the Campaign for Nuclear Disarmament. Jackie Kay originally wanted to be an actress but after a serious road accident requiring a long convalescence, during which she read literature extensively, she began to write. Encouraged by her English teacher and by a writer and artist, the late Alasdair Gray, she decided to become a writer.

Her upbringing was rich in the love and support given to her by her adoptive parents and in the wide social and cultural education they gave her. She describes these seminal experiences in her memoir *Red Dust Road* (Picador Classic edition, 2017) paying a heartfelt tribute to her adoptive parents: 'I am grateful to have grown up in the house with John and Helen Kay, to have had them, great humanitarians that they are, as my mum and dad' (*Red Dust Road*, p. 286).

As she was growing up, she shared the political activities of her parents, joining them on anti-apartheid marches, taking part in the Campaign for Nuclear Disarmament and canvassing with her father who stood as a Communist candidate in election campaigns. She joined the Young Communist League when she was fourteen but left when she was sixteen or seventeen. Although not a member of any political party, she continues to support, among other organisations, Justice, The Scottish Refugee Council, Glasgow Women's Library and The Working Class Movement Library in Salford. She describes living in a very sociable household, where stories, poetry, songs and family memories were shared, and enjoying theatre and opera. International visitors were always welcomed. Holidays in the Highlands and on the island of Mull were special, giving her and her brother an experience of rural and island life and a love of the landscapes of Scotland.

She studied literature at the University of Stirling, graduating in 1983. For three summers during her university years, she worked as a porter in Westminster Hospital, London, and worked temporarily as a cleaner, one of her employers being David Cornwall, whose pen name was John le Carré.

As a child and a student, she was subjected to vicious racial abuse, both physical and verbal. For a time she felt alienated from Scottish life. She needed to find her own voice and to explore her own complex identity as a gay woman of mixed race in the predominantly white, heterosexual and socially conservative Scotland of her childhood and youth. She left Scotland and has lived in Manchester since 1996. She is Professor of Creative Writing at the University of Newcastle and was appointed Chancellor of the University of Salford in 2014. She was appointed Makar (Scotland's National Poet) in 2016, with her tenure ending in 2021. She returns frequently to Scotland to participate in Scotland's cultural life, visiting diverse communities the length and breadth of the country and engaging in a national conversation with the people she meets. In this role, particularly during the Covid-19 pandemic, she has brought comfort and hope to many.

2. IDENTITY

i. Nature and Nurture

In her poem sequence *The Adoption Papers* (*Darling*, pp. 13–40), Jackie Kay gives dramatic and poetic voice to the experiences of her formative years and to her search as an adult for her birth mother. It is an imaginative exploration of the multi-faceted nature of an individual's identity, focusing on the complex inter-relationship between genes (nature) and upbringing (nurture). Although the poems explore the poet's own particular lived experience, they have a universal relevance in a world still riven by racism and social prejudice.

The adopted daughter's story is narrated by three speakers: the adoptive mother, the adopted daughter and the birth mother. Their voices are distinguished typographically: adoptive mother: Gill Sans typeface; daughter: Palatino typeface; and birth mother: Bodoni typeface.

The sequence is in three parts: Part One (1961–62) covers the birth of the daughter, her adoption and the beginnings of her search for her birth mother; Part Two (1967–79) explores her reaction to the revelation that she has been adopted and her experience of racism at school and in the community; Part Three (1980–90) recounts her strong desire to know her family origins, her subsequent search for her birth mother and her hope for a meeting with her.

Written originally as a radio play, the sequence has elements of storytelling, drama and poetry. Each speaker has a distinctive voice and the interplay of the three voices forms a dramatic narrative which expresses their individual perceptions of the circumstances of the daughter's birth, adoption and growing awareness of racial prejudice. The monologues have an immediacy and poetic intensity which have translated successfully to the printed page. The voices of the adoptive mother and daughter are closely based on Helen Kay and Jackie Kay's own lived experience. They speak with a directness and colloquial vigour, at times poignant and sometimes humorous. At the time of writing Jackie Kay knew very little about her birth mother. She, therefore, gives her the imagined voice of a dream mother who expresses her anguish and guilt at having to give up her baby for adoption in emotive language imbued with the shifting imagery of dreams.

The Prologue (p. 15)

The Prologue introduces the three speakers in the following order: the adoptive mother, the daughter and the birth mother. They give voice to the circumstances of the daughter's birth and the possibility of the baby's adoption. Their brief statements set the scene for the sequence of monologues which follow. The adoptive mother speaks of her long-held desire to give birth and the emotional anguish of learning that she was unable to do so. Her husband suggests that they could adopt a child and her immediate reaction reveals her misgivings: 'even in the early sixties there was something scandalous about adopting'. She is fearful of 'bringing up an alien child' whose future might be problematic.

The daughter reveals the facts of her birth: that the forceps delivery had damaged her left cheek and she had spent four months in 'a glass cot' in hospital, a frail infant who might not survive. She attributes her survival to the devotion of her adoptive mother, who visited her faithfully during her four months in hospital.

The birth mother of the poet's imagination briefly speaks her thoughts on the day of her daughter's twenty-sixth birthday. She has kept the baby photo and, aware that she is growing older, she wonders if her daughter imagines her as an ageing woman. Her words imply but do not directly state that she had given up her baby for adoption and convey her continuing sadness and regret.

Part One: 1961–1962

Chapter 1: The Seed (pp. 16–17)

The birth mother expresses her thoughts about the conception of her child, the experience of pregnancy and the desertion of the child's father. She turns over and over in her mind the seemingly chance nature of a 'particular seed to be singled out' for fertilisation and describes the physical discomforts of her situation. Despite the discomfort, she speaks of a certain pride in looking at her swollen belly in the mirror and her strong desire to experience childbirth. She tells us that the father is in Nigeria and has written to say that he cannot return to her and that 'we should have known better'. It is small comfort for a young unmarried woman at a time when societal attitudes to a woman who had a child out of wedlock were harshly disapproving. She acknowledges the powerful attraction the father of her child held for her – 'His eyes intense as whirlwind' – and remembers the music he played her. She speaks with a rueful honesty about her situation and without self-pity. The birth mother reveals a little of the circumstances of the birth – the desertion of the father, giving birth at the age of nineteen and the frailty of her newborn child – but mostly her monologues express her anguish and guilt at having to give up her baby for adoption.

Chapter 2: The Original Birth Certificate (pp. 17–18)

The daughter speaks of her enquiries at Register House in Edinburgh which result in her learning her birth mother's name, her own original name, the name of the hospital and her time of birth. The tone of her account is both matter-of-fact and reflective. There is a degree of bemusement in her words, perhaps hinting that the time of birth makes her special: 'So, so, so, I was a midnight baby after all.' The information is sparse and gives no idea of the birth mother's current circumstances and personality.

The birth mother in her emotionally fragile state after the birth of her daughter has conflicting dreams. In some her baby returns to her but in others she dreams of suffocating her. The frailty of her newborn daughter lying in the 'glass cot' in hospital, however, brings her to an acceptance of reality. She finds herself 'willing life into her' as she watches her daughter 'encased in glass like a museum piece'.

Chapter 3: The Waiting Lists (pp. 19–21)

The adoptive mother recounts the difficulties she and her husband have faced when seeking to adopt a child. She conveys her exasperation and disappointment as one agency after another deems them unsuitable. There is a sense of drama in the telling. She lists the five agencies to whom they have applied and gives reasons for their refusals: they were not church-goers; they did not earn enough; there was a five-year waiting list; there were no babies as opposed to older children available, before building up to the climax of her account: that they would be willing to adopt a baby of colour and, in her words, 'Just like that, the waiting was over'. There is a wry humour in her comment that the child they so much wanted could be five years old by the time they were eligible to adopt and her final words demonstrate how enlightened and generous in spirit they were.

The adoptive mother's gift for developing her experience into a dramatic humorous story is revealed in her monologue describing the visit of an agency official who has come to assess the suitability of the couple and their home. Using colloquial West of Scotland idioms and speech patterns, she brings humour to this difficult situation, describing her efforts to hide any evidence of their communist beliefs and activities. She recounts how she 'put Marx Engels Lenin (no Trotsky) / in the airing cupboard'. She tells how she hid copies of *The Daily Worker* under the sofa and took down a picture of Paul Robeson from the kitchen wall. When the agency worker sits on the sofa, the adoptive mother fears the official will hear the newspapers 'rustle underneath her'. The interplay of the dialogue between the two women is portrayed with a comic brio: 'Well she says, you have an interesting home'. The adoptive mother feels she is 'on the home run' until the agency woman notices a red ribbon with twenty world peace badges hanging on the wall. The official asks her if she is against nuclear weapons and, deciding to throw caution to the wind and give an honest answer, she exclaims, 'To Hell with this [...] / I'd like this baby to live in a nuclear free world'. To her surprise the agency woman agrees with her: 'I'm all for peace myself she says, / and sits down for another cup of coffee'. A humorous anti-climax to a well-told story. These two monologues have a dramatic immediacy and a colloquial directness.

Chapter 4: Baby Lazarus (pp. 21–23)

Her euphoria is short-lived, however, when the social worker tells her that the baby she can adopt is not healthy and the adoption papers cannot be signed until the doctor has deemed the baby is well. Her monologue gives us these facts and, although very upset by this news, she tells herself not to 'get overwrought' accepting that she cannot be a mother until she has signed the adoption papers. By December she is more hopeful, telling of her excitement at seeing the baby for the first time. By March the baby has passed the medical tests and can now be adopted. Her reaction to this news is one of exasperation at the short notice they have been given to collect the baby but also reveals her underlying anxiety. Her down to

earth account of the adoption process has the authenticity of
lived experience and establishes her as a warm, caring and
outgoing person.

In contrast, the birth mother speaks of returning to Aberdeen
bereft after giving up her baby for adoption. She watches the
'frigid earth' of winter from the train window, describing in
a poignant metaphor the train as a 'rocking cradle'. She is
intensely aware of a case of infanticide featured in a newspaper headline: 'MOTHER DROWNS BABY IN THE CLYDE'.
In her imagination she sees the words 'MOTHER GIVES BABY
AWAY' written on her forehead in 'thin ink'. Once home she
tells how she buried her daughter's baby clothes in the garden.
Looking out her window a week later she imagines the ground
is swelling with 'the promise of a crop'; that she hears her
baby crying. She gives her daughter a burial service and curses
herself for 'digging a pit for my baby', but in the night she
dreams of a resurrection, that her 'baby Lazarus' has come
back to life and is suckling at her breast. Her words powerfully evoke her emotional trauma as she faces the reality of
giving up her baby for adoption.

Chapter 5: The Tweed Hat Dream (pp. 24–25)

The adoptive mother's common sense and realistic attitude
towards the difficulties she and her husband have faced and
continue to face do not, however, insulate her from underlying
subconscious fears. She dreams that her daughter's birth
mother has turned up at her door 'with a tweed hat on'. The
birth mother asks to see her baby daughter: 'She comes in
swift / as wind in a storm', picks up the baby and 'strokes her
cheeks endlessly'. The adoptive mother goes downstairs to
put the kettle on and arrange a plate of biscuits, but she is
apprehensive. The birth mother stays upstairs with the baby
for a long time and, alarmed, the adoptive mother is 'pounding

the stairs / like thunder' to find that 'Her tweed hat / is in the cot. That is all'. The dream has become a nightmare ending like a bad fairy tale. The child has been taken, spirited away. The juxtaposition of the welcoming domestic scene and the disappearance of the 'lightning white' mother with the 'soft Highland voice' brings into sharp focus the birth mother's trauma and the emotional stress experienced by the adoptive mother.

Part Two: 1967–1971

Chapter 6: The Telling Part (pp. 26–28)

This chapter begins with the daughter's realisation that she has been adopted. The repeated statements all beginning with 'ma mammy' culminate in her statement that her 'mammy says she's no really ma mammy / (just kid on)'. Her adoptive mother had anticipated the moment of her daughter's realisation that she was adopted, but when the inevitable question came, 'Mammy why aren't you and me the same colour', she finds it very difficult to tell her the truth as gently as possible, stating 'all my planned speech / went out the window' and says bluntly *'I'm not your real mother'*. Her daughter's response is heartening:

> But I love my mammy whether she's real or no
> [...]
> She took me when I'd nowhere to go
> my mammy is the best mammy in the world OK.

That assertive 'OK' is defying anyone to say otherwise. She describes her fears in the night but demonstrates her resilience by telling us that a day after the telling she 'got my guinea pig' and forgot all about it. The exchanges between the

adoptive mother and her daughter are humorous and poignant
and demonstrate the strong emotional bond between them.
She recognises that her adopted daughter has the right to
know the truth about her adoption and reassures her that 'her
other mother' will remember her daughter's birthdays 'all
the way up to / god knows when'.

The young daughter creates a vivid picture of a domestic
scene in which her adoptive mother is singing as she is making
soup. The child's lively narration illustrates the warmth of
their relationship and her mother's sense of fun:

> Mammy's face is cherries.
> She is stirring the big pot of mutton soup
> [...]
> I am up to her apron.
> I jump on her feet and grab her legs
> like a huge pair of trousers,
> she walks round the kitchen lifting me up.

The capers end when she falls off her mother's feet causing
her mother to fall. Her gift for dramatic invention has her
mother still singing as she lies on the floor. Her description
of her mother's skin as 'toffee stuck to the floor. / And her
bones are all scattered like toys' conveys her sense of shock
that her mother is vulnerable and can be hurt.

The adoptive mother's forthright contradiction of the belief
that having an adopted child is not like having one's own child
challenges this assumption. She says movingly:

> she's my child, I have told her stories
> wept at her losses, laughed at her pleasures,
> she is mine.
> [...]
> all this umbilical knot business is nonsense

By speaking her thoughts directly, she takes us into her confidence reinforcing our perceptions of her as a woman who is strong in her practical and emotional support for her daughter, sensitive to her feelings and the feelings of the birth mother and not afraid to voice her own fears and misgivings.

The final narrative in this chapter is spoken by the daughter who, as she is growing up, becomes aware of cultures different from the local West of Scotland culture she experiences in school and in the community. She does not identify with white pop culture, finding pleasure and enrichment instead in African American music. She and her friend mime to the songs of Bessie Smith, the Empress of the Blues, and Pearl Bailey and practise ballroom dancing which, in the 'swinging sixties' and seventies, was, as she comments, 'dead old-fashioned'.

Chapter 7: Black Bottom (pp. 29–32)

This chapter focuses on the issue of racism. The adoptive mother condemns the racial prejudice of others, asserting that 'colour matters to the nutters', but recognises that it matters very much to her daughter. Her daughter narrates her reactions to the racial prejudice she suffered as a child, telling of repeated name-calling and physical bullying. She recreates a specific incident, vividly quoting the verbal and physical exchanges between herself and the bullies: 'I chase his *Sambo Sambo* all the way from the school gate. / A fistful of anorak – What did you call me? Say that again.' Her narration conveys the harsh reality of the boy's behaviour and her visceral reaction to it. Her teacher's response to the situation is deeply troubling. She views it as no more than a fight between two children and condemns the daughter, saying 'In a few years time you'll be a juvenile delinquent' and patronisingly tells her to look up the meaning of the phrase in a dictionary.

Her mother continues her train of thought, explaining that she may not be constantly thinking about the issue of colour but when her daughter is racially abused by other children or adults, she robustly defends her. She is her daughter's champion. She understands the difficulties and hurt her daughter experiences and acknowledges that it is often hard to find the words 'that will comfort', demonstrating the care and concern she has for her daughter. She is stalwart in her support for her and by her actions shows her understanding and empathy when words are inadequate. The daughter relates a further incident in which the insensitivity and prejudice of a particular teacher is highlighted. When practising for a school show, the daughter cannot get the dance steps right. The teacher remarks 'I thought / you people had it in your blood'. Cut to the quick, the daughter describes her embarrassment and hurt: 'My skin is hot as burning coal' and asks the question '*What Is In My Blood?*'. Her teacher's insensitive ignorant remarks sink deep into the young girl's mind. They are more insidious than the bullying of her peers. It takes the intervention of her adoptive father at a parents' night to bring a halt to the teacher's cruel remarks – and even that is not enough.

As she grows up, she imagines film stars whose identities she might try out: Bette Davis, Katherine Hepburn, Elizabeth Taylor, humorously pondering the idea of adopting a role or having a role model. It is the beginning of her desire to be an actress but, unsuccessful in her audition for a part in a stage adaptation of *The Prime of Miss Jean Brodie*, she wryly comments that she did not get the part even though she had 'been acting longer / than Beverley Innes. So I have. Honest.' Her humorous confession of her disappointment and pique reveals her growing self-awareness. As she is growing up, she becomes more and more aware of injustice beyond her own immediate experiences, citing the brutal injustices inflicted on people of colour but particularly on African Americans, quoting the case of Angela Davis who was wrongly accused of murder. She identifies with her not just for the injustice done to her but because she realises that she looks like Angela Davis with skin the same colour and 'big hair'. Her father tries to reassure her that Angela Davis will not be found guilty and condemned to the electric chair. She also becomes aware of the gulf between the broadening of her own cultural awareness and the culture of her school mates, who ask 'Who's she?' when she mentions Angela Davis.

In this chapter there is the continuing focus on the attitudes of others to people of colour. Her birth mother comments on people's reaction to her relationship with a black man, describing with vivid imagery how 'heads turned / like horses, folk stood like trees / their eyes fixed on us' when they walked out together. She burned with discomfort and embarrassment but their passion for each other overcame this very public expression of disapproval and suspicion. She remembers looking at her daughter in her 'glass cot' seeking signs of resemblance to her birth father. It is a poignant commentary on the deep emotional damage she has suffered.

Part Three: 1980–1990

Chapter 8: Generations (pp. 33–35)

This chapter begins with the birth mother's memories of the scandal of her pregnancy, of the voices of the local gossips, which she likens to the relentlessly loud penetrating sound of a pneumatic drill, and her fears that her daughter, now nineteen, will try to contact her.

Her daughter repeats the words of the prologue in which she tells of her difficult birth and the devoted attention of her adoptive mother who visited her faithfully in hospital during the first four months of her life. She returns to the idea of blood lines, a person's genetic inheritance. She is unable to answer medical professionals' questions about her biological family's history and is irked by their enquiries,

their insistence that this matters. She wants to know, never-
theless, her genetic origins. She wonders who her grand-
mothers were and what their lives were like.

She imagines that her birth mother knows that her daughter
often thinks of her in the dawn or as darkness falls and
portrays her dream mother inhabiting her daughter's dreams,
entering her bed, murmuring *'you'll never really know your
mother'*. Her mother's words are unsettling and uncanny,
suggesting the psychological complexity of her daughter's
feelings about her biological mother and reveal the power of
the daughter's imagination in articulating them.

In her subsequent monologue the daughter lists the few
facts she knows about her mother, but she cannot visualise
her face. Her monologue is punctuated by interjections from
her imagined mother. Both mother and daughter try to visualise each other but no matter how fast she runs after her
mother, she cannot reach her. Her mother remains an unsettling elusive presence who is faceless and who 'never weeps'.
Just one meeting with her would comfort the daughter, would
enable her to hear her mother's voice and observe how she
moves her hands when she speaks. The juxtaposition of the
two women's visualisations of each other gives poignant
expression to the long-term emotional consequences of adoption which deeply affect both the birth mother and her child.

Chapter 9: The Phone Call (pp. 36–37)

The daughter relates in a naturalistic narrative the phone
conversation she has with her maternal grandmother and one
of her aunts after hesitating to do so for four months. They
quickly realise that she is Elizabeth's daughter, not a former
work colleague of Elizabeth. Their response is friendly and
the aunt agrees to give Elizabeth her daughter's phone number,
but is not willing to give her niece Elizabeth's number. She
assures her, however, that Elizabeth will write to her. The

effect of the daughter's search and subsequent contact with her grandmother and aunt is unsettling for the adoptive mother, who is concerned that her daughter will be hurt if she meets her birth mother. She admits that she feels hurt by her daughter's actions but chides herself with characteristic and forthright honesty that she is being 'Daft. Getting myself into a tizzy'.

Chapter 10: The Meeting Dream (pp. 37–40)

In her reaction to seeing the photograph of her birth mother, the daughter contrasts it with her imagined image of her. She describes her dream of their meeting in her birth mother's living room, their walk by 'the shore' and return to her mother's house. Their meeting is tense with suppressed emotion. She asked her mother if their meeting is how she imagined it. Her reply is blunt: 'I never imagined it. / [...] It would have driven me mad imagining, / 26 years is a long time'. Kay uses powerful imagery to convey the emotional strain of their imagined meeting. The daughter's eyes 'are stones washed over and over'; her hands 'are awkward as rocks'. Her dreams of her birth mother are painful and express her misgivings about her search for her: 'One dream cuts another open like a gutted fish'. This violent image reinforces the depth of her distress, and the message of her dreams and imaginings seems to be, having once met, they will not meet again; that 'she is too many imaginings to be flesh and blood'. There is a sense of despair in her words.

The poem sequence does not end, however, in a mood of despair. It ends as it began with three short monologues. There is a change in the order of speakers, the final words being spoken by the daughter and not by the birth mother as in the prologue. The adoptive mother speaks first, reflecting that she had told her daughter the truth about her adoption as soon as her daughter had asked about her different colour and had reassured her that, if she ever wanted to find her birth mother, she would respect that desire and would not stand in the way. Such a need to explore one's origins was natural. She speaks of the rock-solid bond between them in her forthright way: 'We're on the wavelength so we are. / [...] Closer than blood. / Thicker than water. Me and my daughter.' The imagined birth mother speaks of going out before dawn and throwing her baby daughter's photo down an old well near her home. It may be a dream and her actions could readily be inter-preted as a rejection of her daughter. Her words, however, indicate perhaps more of an acceptance that her baby has grown up and lives her own independent life. By imagining her mother losing her fear and being freed from deeply troubling dreams, the poet is suggesting that her mother has found a peace of mind which had eluded her for so many years. In the final monologue the daughter tells us that she is hoping her mother will write to her. She awaits with anxious antici-pation 'the crash of the letter box / then the soft thud of words on the matt'. There is humour in her 'fantasising the colour of her paper / whether she'll underline First Class / or have a large circle over her "i"s.'

The poem sequence does not end with the delivery of a letter or the promise of a meeting, but it leaves us with a sense of hope that the outcome of her daughter's search for her birth mother will be a positive one for all three women.

ii. Family Poems

Many of Jackie Kay's poems portray individual members of her adoptive and birth families and her complex relationship with them. Her strong enduring bond with her adoptive parents has inspired a number of poems such as 'George Square', 'Lucozade' and 'Thirty-Five'. In an interview with the *Scottish Review of Books* in 2016 she paid tribute to her adoptive parents:

> For me, my parents enabled me, and I wouldn't be sat here
> if it wasn't for them. I feel like they opened doors rather than
> pushed me through them and I didn't feel indoctrinated. I
> don't think I would have been so strong-willed had I been
> constrained. It's a massive privilege to be with these parents.

'George Square' (*Darling*, p. 187) expresses the poet's admiration and affection for her late parents who were still politically engaged and active in old age. The first verse describes her parents coping with some of the physical challenges of ageing and, by quoting her mother's words, 'What a pair the two of us are!', the poet conveys the humour and resilience of her mother. Beginning with the colloquial phrase 'And off they went', the poet suggests that they will not let age dampen their resolve 'to march against the war in Iraq'. Kay continues in colloquial vein in the next line, commenting 'him with his plastic hips and her with her arthritis', and by so doing engages us, the listener or reader, in the conversation. In the last four lines she describes the gathering of the protesters in George Square more formally using the image of the banners which 'waved at each other like old friends' to emphasise her parents' commitment to the cause of peace over many years. The final line of the poem with the interjection 'for pity's sake' suggests the poet's strong conviction that it is a sad reflection of the parlous state of the world which still cannot achieve lasting peace and a plea for the end of all war in solidarity with her indomitable parents.

In **'Lucozade'** (*Darling*, p. 138) she describes visiting her mother in hospital. She was a young girl of sixteen, afraid her mother would die. The words of the poem are a blend of the poet's adult voice recollecting the visit and her teenage voice narrating her experience and reactions to seeing her mother on 'a high bed' in the hospital ward. She repeats the phrase 'sad chrysanthemums', suggesting that the flowers

are wilting and becoming a symbol of decay and death. The
poem not only describes the shock of seeing her mother but
also conveys the personality of her mother expressively and
with humour. Her mother's ironic questions, her humorous
commands and her idiosyncratic remarks may be partly the
result of her operation or treatment but they strongly suggest
a person who faces her hospital experience with spirit and
humour. There is something indomitable about her. Despite
her groggy state her mother commands her daughter not to
bring Lucozade, 'Orange nostalgia', she calls it, or 'maga-
zines'. She makes demands: 'Tell your father to bring a luxury'
and 'Tell him: stop the neighbours coming'. She wants to know
where the luxuries are: 'the big brandy, the generous gin, the
Bloody Mary, / the biscuit tin, the chocolate gingers, the dirty
big meringue'. The phrase 'says she' suggests her daughter's
bemusement that her mother has not lost her spirit and wit.
It's a way of saying colloquially that her mother is 'Some
woman!'.

The last two stanzas describe the euphoria of relief the poet
feels when she realises her mother will not die but has recovered enough to wave from her hospital bed. It is a cathartic
moment for the sixteen-year-old poet – an epiphany. Her senses
heightened after the trauma of her mother's hospitalisation,
the sight of her mother waving becomes for her a precious
moment, a beautiful almost heavenly vision. The metaphor
'dandelion hours' is enigmatic, perhaps suggesting that like
a dandelion head swept away by the wind, her visit to her
mother is brief but precious or that for the poet as a young
girl, her mother's experience in hospital has made her aware
of mortality, of the transience of life.

As one of the poets commissioned by the Royal Society of
Literature to write a sonnet inspired by a Shakespeare sonnet,
Jackie Kay chose Sonnet 11 as her inspiration. **'Thirty-Five'**
(*Bantam*, p. 53) is a tribute to her adoptive mother, Helen

Kay. A Shakespearian sonnet has a fixed form of fourteen lines consisting of three quatrains (four-line sections) and a final couplet. It is usually rhymed *abab cdcd efef gg*. Each quatrain develops a particular stage of the poet's argument with the final couplet either bringing the argument to a conclusion or subverting it with a contradiction. Shakespeare's poem does not directly explore the theme of love but rather concentrates on the speaker, the poet's persona, urging the object of his love to have children.

In the first quatrain he tells his addressee that, although youth wanes swiftly, his beauty and youthful vigour will live on, will grow anew in the 'fresh blood' of his children. To bestow such gifts on the next generation, the speaker suggests in the second quatrain, will bring 'wisdom, beauty and increase'. Without these qualities there is only 'folly, age and cold decay'. He seems to suggest that if everyone was not 'minded' to procreate, the 'times should cease'; that the world would end. In the third quatrain he develops his argument into stark advice to his addressee. For those not best endowed by Nature to acquire wisdom and longevity, he has a bleak deterministic message: they will be preordained to die, to 'perish' without offspring. He, therefore, exhorts the addressee to 'cherish' this 'bounteous gift' of beauty, wisdom and vigour which Nature has given him. In the final couplet the speaker concludes his argument with a metaphorical flourish. Nature has printed her seal on the object of his love, who, in the creating of the next generation, will print more copies of himself. By idealising this individual, the speaker is paying him the highest compliment. The one he loves has been specially endowed by Nature to stand out from the 'common herd'.

Shakespeare's sonnet does not provide a context. We do not know the identity of the addressee; there is no narrative; the particular circumstances which gave rise to the sentiments of the poem are not revealed. Kay's sonnet, on the other hand, describes a specific incident. Each poem, however, expresses the intense feelings each speaker has for the addressee. Kay's sonnet is looser in form than the Shakespearian sonnet and has a less regular rhyme scheme. The addressee is not an unknown idealised lover but rather the speaker's mother, who has suddenly fallen ill and has been taken to hospital. The first six lines describe the situation and express the daughter's admiration for her mother's spirit and courage and relief that she has quickly recovered. In contrast to the sombre observations of Shakespeare's poetic persona on the fragility of life and the inevitability of ageing, the Kay poem is optimistic in tone celebrating the new lease of life the application of the 'saline drip' and the 'subcut' have given her mother, without shying away from the physical realities of illness and treatment. She contrasts the bleak chill of winter outside the hospital with the warmth of her mother's personality, her life-giving wit and wisdom despite her illness and the procedures she endures. For the poet, her mother's speedy recovery and resilience after the shock of her sudden illness move her deeply. Her mother's illness has brought into sharp focus the strength of the love her mother has for her. Without it 'nothing could ever be well'. Kay has taken the idea, expressed in Shakespeare's sonnet, that there is a natural imperative to pass on one's superior genes to the next generation, and radically altered it to assert that her mother's love is the 'bounteous gift' bestowed on her from 'early in this life'. The line 'The more you give the more you will have to cherish' suggests that her daughter's life has been greatly enriched by the love and support of her mother and she in turn reciprocates that love. In a dramatic declaration the daughter asserts that 'If I could offer you my veins, I'd gladly use a knife'. It is strikingly different from Shakespeare's poetic persona's exhortation to pass on family blood lines. The final couplet refers to the kiss of love which has sealed their love for each other and to which they will hold fast no matter what storms life may bring.

In her poem **'85th Birthday Poem for Dad'** (*Fiere*, pp. 44–45), the poet pays tribute to her adoptive father, John Kay. She expresses her thoughts and feelings as she watches 'a large red sun' slowly setting behind a cliff in Erin Bay on the Isle of Man. She compares the sun to 'a ball in a penalty' and the moon, suddenly appearing through the clouds, to the ball which is 'lobbed' into the net. This footballing imagery prepares us for her memory of her father who had played centre forward in a team in New Zealand and the observation that her mother had never watched him play. That this was his 'only bugbear' with his wife in the fifty years of their marriage gives us an immediate and engaging insight into an important aspect of his earlier life and the strength of her parents' relationship.

Extending the footballing imagery in the second stanza, the poet suggests the passing of time: that while the setting of the sun and the rising of the moon remain constant 'in the sky's great pitch', human life moves on. Remembering her father is both a celebration of his life and a way of holding on, of cherishing her memories of him. She remembers how active he was: so full of life dancing 'across the ballroom floor / like Fred Astaire' and climbing Munros. Raising her half pint glass to him she drinks an 'extra wee half' of whisky, 'a *Port Ellen*', which happens to have her mother's name.

In the third stanza she refers to the traditional Scottish custom of drinking a half pint of beer and a nip of whisky, a half and a half, remembering that her father would say in Scots 'a hauf and a hauf'. By toasting his health, the poet is inviting us to share vicariously in the celebration. She imagines that if he were with her on the Isle of Man, he would be making associations: the Isle of Man, Thomas Paine's *Rights of Man,* that 'Nobility is not hereditary, aye'. By alluding to her father's social and political beliefs she is paying tribute to him as a man who believed in social justice for all regardless of class or privilege and had worked tirelessly in that cause. She expresses regret that he is not with her on his birthday but raises a glass to the man who played football, climbed mountains, danced like Fred Astaire, sustained his loving relationship with his wife for over fifty years and believed strongly in the right of all human beings to a decent and fulfilling life. Jackie Kay's poem is a warm and fitting tribute to a remarkable man.

In her memoir *Red Dust Road*, Kay describes the sense of 'aloneness' she feels as an adopted person. It troubles her that this feeling at her 'heart's core' persists despite the unstinting love her adoptive parents, her son and her lover give her. She feels a great need to know her birth parents. She acknowledges that for adopted persons, finding and meeting their birth parents can be either a joyful or a profoundly distressing experience and that in searching for her birth parents, whose life stories she has created in her imagination since she was a girl, she is exploring the makings of her own identity, her own story.

Having traced her birth mother, she meets her for the first time in a hotel in Milton Keynes in 1991. In the weeks after their first meeting, she felt 'jangled and upset' by the complex emotions it had engendered. She describes her feelings as a kind of grief for 'the imaginary mother' she had carried in her head for so long rather than the real Elizabeth who had not had an easy life and had suffered much.

'Keeping Orchids' (*Darling*, p. 86) gives poetic expression to this first meeting. It is a painful experience for both women. The poet uses the images of the orchids her birth mother gave her and of her own and Elizabeth's troubled hands as symbols of the complex emotions they both feel. It is not a joyful meeting. Kay articulates her own feelings but finds it hard to read her mother's as Elizabeth 'tells the story of her life'.

   The first six verses give an account of her care for the orchids in the twelve days since she brought them home. She wishes to keep them alive and fresh for as long as possible, carrying them home 'like a baby in a shawl', the simile emphasising that they are precious to her. Some of the buds remain 'closed as secrets', the phrase an intimation of the areas of her life her mother will not reveal. Twice the glass carafe which holds the orchids falls over and the poet rearranges them 'with troubled hands'. The 'upset orchids', a transferred epithet, and the over-toppled carafe become a poetic shorthand for the poet's troubled emotions. The closed buds suggest the keeping of secrets about her life, which Elizabeth will not reveal. The phrase 'All the broken waters' suggests what has gone before in her life and the rearranging of the orchids 'with troubled hands' suggests the poet's need to understand the as yet unknown aspects of her mother's life. The phrase 'Twelve days later' in verse six emphasises the effort the poet has made to keep the orchids alive and signals the intensifying of her emotions. Just as the orchids are fading, her mother's 'face is fading fast'. There is anguish in her statement that 'my mother's hands are all I have': that 'her voice rushes / through a tunnel the other way from home'. Trying to remember her mother's face, she lists the clothes she was wearing and mentions the digital watch which had belonged to her daughter. In verse nine the poet returns to the image of the orchids which 'hang their heads, // and suddenly grow old', symbolising the poet's realisation that her mother is no longer young and testifying to the fact that they have indeed met. In verses ten and eleven it is her mother's, not her own, 'troubled hands' she describes, which 'fold and unfold a green carrier bag as she tells / the story of her life'. The poet uses a series of metaphors to describe her mother's account of her life. It is 'Compressed', 'Airtight', 'A sad square': it does not reveal enough to bring comfort to her daughter, hungry for emotional

connection and revelation. In verse thirteen the poet employs
the metaphor of a door opening and closing to suggest that,
although she has achieved a first meeting with her mother, so
much of her remains hidden and closed to her. The personification of time 'outside waiting' reinforces the poet's awareness that her mother is no longer young: that there is not
unlimited time in which to get to know her. She further reinforces the idea of the inexorable march of time and ageing in
the metaphor of the cold 'draught in my winter room'.

The final lines of the poem return to the orchids which, the
poet suggests, can live longer if doused in boiling water or
have their stems cut with a sharp knife, drastic treatment for
such delicate flowers. These final lines suggest, perhaps, the
poet's strong unsettling emotions which the meeting has
aroused in her. In striving to keep the orchids alive as long
as possible, she is holding on to her hope of really knowing
her mother despite the pain experienced by them both. The
poem is at once a poignant expression of deep emotion and an
acknowledgement of the painful realities of their first meeting.

In her memoir *Red Dust Road*, the poet recounts her meeting
with her aunts, her birth mother's sisters, who told her that
her mother had grown up with her grandparents. Although
the poet never met her grandmother, she gained an impression of her from the memories of her aunts. They described
her as a fierce woman who would defend anyone she loved but
had disapproved of Elizabeth's relationship with a black man
and had insisted that she give up her baby for adoption.

The poem **'My Grandmother'** (*Darling*, p. 12) prefaces *The
Adoption Papers*. It is not the portrayal of the poet's actual
grandmother but of a grandmother of the imagination. It is
an expression of the poet's strong feelings about the societal
prejudices which influence an individual's attitudes to race
and colour. The first section could be described as a praise

poem in which the grandmother's appearance and character
are defined in terms of the land to which she belongs. Her
bearing and demeanour are compared to a Scottish pine which
grows tall and strong in a harsh environment, a symbol of
strength and endurance. The metaphor 'Her face is ploughed
land' suggests the lines on her face are like furrows formed
after ploughing but it is not a negative image, suggesting
perhaps the experience of age rather than the unploughed field
of youth. She has piercing blue eyes and wears 'with the
zeal of an Amazon' a tartan shawl, a marker of the clan to
which she belongs suggesting a fierce pride in her ancestry.
(The Amazons were a race of warrior women whom Herodotus,
the early Greek historian, alleged came from Scythia. They
were mythologised in the Greek legends of Hercules and
Theseus and the city of Troy.) In a reference to the Highland
Clearances of the nineteenth century, when landowners, moti-
vated by greed to clear the crofting land for more profitable
sheep farming, forced crofters to give up their crofts and move
to barren land by the seashore or emigrate, the grandmother
is likened to a woman whose love of and identification with
her ancestral land would not allow her to give up her croft
even under the most brutal circumstances. Strong-willed
and determined, she holds to her Gaelic tongue and only
uses English when forced to. Rather than an individual, she
seems more of an archetype who stands for a line of strong
women, indomitable in spirit, hardened but not defeated by
harsh experience.

The poem turns, however, in the following two lines, to a
negative portrayal of the grandmother, who sits by the fire
swearing 'There'll be no darkie baby in this house'. Her brutal
declaration, devoid of understanding or compassion, speaks
of an ingrained racial prejudice. It is a cruel irony that, as a
descendant of victims of a landlord's inhumanity, she will not

countenance or welcome a baby of colour into her family or home, referring contemptuously to the child as a 'darkie baby'.

The final section of the poem exactly repeats the first two lines but the concluding three lines create harsher images. Her 'loose bun' has become 'a ball of steel wool', her facial expression icy and her blue eyes hard as stone.

This portrayal of the grandmother illustrates the complex nature of racial prejudice in an individual who in many ways can be admired but has been conditioned by the ingrained societal prejudices of her time to refuse to accept a black child as a welcomed and loved addition to her family.

In contrast, Kay's poem **'My Grandmother's Houses'** (*Darling*, pp. 45–46) is an affectionate portrayal of her adoptive father's mother. It simultaneously recreates her childhood experiences of her grandmother and voices her adult perceptions of her. The three sections of the poem describe a different house, each flat reflecting different aspects of her life, work and personality. The final three lines of the third section tell us that she has moved to a ground-floor flat in her high rise where the view from her living room window is of ambulances racing to Glasgow Royal Infirmary. This structure enables the poet to create a vivid, memorable portrait of her. The first section describes the tenement flat with her granny's bedroom's idiosyncratic clutter. The bedroom is the young Jackie Kay's favourite room, housing a hoard of interesting things such as old newspapers and various gifts accumulated over the years. In her young child's voice, the poet describes, with humour and a degree of exaggeration, the effort of climbing over the accumulated clutter to get to the bed as 'harder than the school's obstacle course'. She reads newspaper stories of events she does not yet understand and expresses her mother's exasperation at the hoarding of the grandmother but to the young girl it is a treasure trove, a source of endless interest.

When her grandmother gets notice to move to a high-rise block, she does not want to go. The poet describes her forthright objections to being moved. She is 'hopping mad'. The flat is her home and she is part of a community. With a child's perception of the everyday details of her granny's life – the newsagents which sells hazelnut toffees and her *Daily Record* which she chews over 'for ages' – Jackie Kay builds up a humorous and engaging portrayal of her granny whose metaphorical 'chewing' of the newspaper becomes a literal chewing of the toffees which the young child remembers stuck to her false teeth. And it is through the accumulation of small details of her grandmother's life that we feel we have been given the privilege of knowing her.

Her move to the high flat points to the huge social changes brought about by the tearing down of the tenements in Glasgow and other cities. With the benefit of hindsight, we now know how damaging the wholesale dislocation of working-class communities was to people's lives and the alienation such radical changes caused to many.

In the second section of the poem Kay tells us her grandmother keeps busy making what seems to her young self 'endless pots of vegetable soup' as gradually she begins to like the modern facilities of the flat. But she 'still doesn't settle down' and goes out to clean people's houses 'even at seventy'. We learn she is a devout Christian and Kay describes, from her perspective as a young child, how her granny would be 'dragging' her along to the strange place 'where the air / is trapped and ghosts sit at the altar'. She is uncomfortable in the church environment describing the worshippers as 'A flock of women in coats and fussy hats / flapping over me like missionaries'. The metaphor of the women described as a flock of birds reveals the young girl's sensitivity and discomfort at being made a fuss of by women who find her, as a mixed-race child, a curiosity or a novelty. The final irreverent, alliterative lines of this section, 'and that is that, / until the next time God grabs me in Glasgow with Gran', suggest that the young Jackie Kay is enjoying playing with language and signals that, although she is sceptical about religious belief, she accepts that going to church with her grandmother is, no matter how uncomfortable she feels, an important part of the time she spends with her.

The third section indicates the passing of time. At the age of seven the poet is almost the same height as her grandmother. She describes her granny rushing her 'down the High Street' to 'her cleaning house'. She vividly recreates a particular experience with a wealth of description and comment. The contrast with her grandmother's flat could not be greater. She relates that 'The hall is huge. / Rooms lead off like an octopus's arms', the simile emphasising the child's perception of a large house with many rooms. The grand piano with its lid open is described metaphorically as 'a one-winged creature'. Out of boredom, as her grandmother polishes for what seems like hours, she picks out the traditional tune 'oh can you wash a sailor's shirt' several times on the piano until her grandmother reprimands her with the words 'I told you don't touch anything'. The owner of the house, alerted by the sound of the piano, appears and the dialogue between the two women upsets the child, the whole exchange highlighting the social gap between them and the condescending attitude of the owner, the 'posh one', who asks the young Jackie Kay to sing for her. She obliges and sings 'Kumbaya' which charms the owner who patronises her with her remarks of 'beautiful child, skin the colour of café au lait'. Her grandmother apologises for her granddaughter's behaviour which emphasises again the inferior social position of her grandmother who is told to get back to her work. There is an implied criticism of ingrained class divisions and racial stereotyping in the society in which Jackie Kay was growing up. As they return to her grandmother's high-rise flat, she is very aware of her grandmother's ageing, describing with the bluntness of an observant child that her back was bent 'like the hunchback of Notre Dame' and quoting with a touch of humour her admonition to 'Sit up straight'. Her insistence on good posture in her grandchild crouched over a comic further reinforces our impression of her as a no-nonsense caring granny.

The third last line of the poem tells us that her grandmother has moved to a ground-floor flat in a high-rise. The inference is that she has become too frail to continue to live on the twenty-fourth floor. The two final lines echo the first two lines of the poem. The view from her tenement flat was of a cemetery, and from her ground-floor flat, of ambulances racing to Glasgow Royal Infirmary. It is a sombre ending to a poem which pays an affectionate, unsentimental tribute to the life of this spirited, hard-working and devout woman.

Two poems which complement one another are 'Bantam' and 'Private Joseph Kay', written in memory of the poet's grandfather.

'Bantam' (*Bantam*, p. 3) captures her adoptive father's words as he remembers the small men, one of whom was his father, Joseph Kay, who formed bantam battalions in the First World War. His father joined the Highland Light Infantry in Glasgow and fought and was captured at the Somme. With an economy of words in the Scots/English of the West of Scotland, he encapsulates a particular aspect of the history of the First World War: the dropping of the height restriction for young recruits, scarcely more than boys, who were sent to fight in France and Belgium. Because of their small stature (under five foot three inches) they were named 'Bantams', 'wee men named after / sma' chickens'. The army's need for fighting men is concisely expressed in the demotic phrase 'That needy, fir soldiers' and is followed by the more formal summative statement 'so small men came to war'. Throughout the poem

the repeated references to the youth and small stature of the
recruits emphasise both their willingness to join up and their
vulnerability.

The latter part of the poem focuses on Jackie Kay's grandfather's particular experience of war. Shrapnel 'frae the
Somme' lodged in his arm and as a prisoner of war his weight
dropped. It was not until many years later that the shrapnel
became dislodged and 'shot' from his arm. By using her father's
words, expressed in remembrance of his father, the poet shapes
a moving tribute to her grandfather and all the 'bantams' who
fought in the First World War.

'Private Joseph Kay' (*Bantam*, pp. 4–5) is written in the
form of couplets which build up a picture of the poet's grandfather who lost friends and workmates in the First World War.
The poet recounts one of her father's memories of his father
whom he remembers as a quiet man who 'never, ever raised
his voice in anger', who was shy and a 'bit withdrawn', perhaps
as a result of his experiences as a soldier and prisoner of war.
We learn that he worked as a tram driver rising at dawn,
'Polishing the brass buttons of his tram driver's uniform'
before starting his shift, the description indicating a pride in
his appearance and work. We learn he was a singer of both
popular Scots songs and operatic arias. The question 'What
was that Wagner aria?' suggests perhaps her father searching
his memories of his father singing and segues into the poet's
appreciation of her father's singing, an inherited gift from
his father. In the line 'Ballads slide down the years' she
focuses on the passing down of musical prowess and tradition
from father to son, who at the age of ninety is 'still singing
his father' in song and memory. The line 'There's life in
the old dog yet' perhaps expresses her father's wry, self-
deprecating but life-affirming assertion of vitality and energy
despite his ninety years. Her final picture of her grandfather
as she imagines him beginning to sing expresses her affection

for and pride in her grandfather and father and testifies to the power and importance of family memories.

A sense of the inevitable march of time permeates the poem entitled **'Piano 4 p.m.'** *(Darling*, pp. 191–92). It describes a domestic scene capturing the immediacy of the poet's experience on the page. Her son is practising his scales on the piano then progresses to playing a classical piece, 'Arioso in F', while she is preparing dinner. Her description of his playing parallels her detailed account of her preparations for the meal. His playing triggers her memories of the past and thoughts of the future when her 'boy' will become a man. As the music flows, 'sweeps and turns', 'yearns and swings', the different moods it evokes have a powerful emotional effect on her. Holding her wooden spoon 'mid-air / like a proud conductor', she celebrates her son's playing and is moved to tears by its power.

The poem captures a precious moment in the poet's family life and expresses both her joy in his prowess and an acute awareness of the passing of time.

While many of Jackie Kay's poems explore her own family relationships, she also creates other voices often of vulnerable and marginalised individuals whose family relationships are under strain. In her poem **'Bed'** *(Darling*, pp. 148–49) she uses the dramatic monologue form to convey the stark realities of extreme old age. The speaker is an elderly bed-bound woman, completely dependent on her daughter for her care. She voices her thoughts and feelings in a colloquial Scots which is direct, expressive and sometimes bleakly humorous. Her words describe with a raw honesty the physical ravages of old age and the guilt and frustration it causes. She feels her dependent state keenly confined to her 'big blastit bed / year in, year oot', the alliteration and the repetitive phrases giving force to her feelings of frustration. Having to rely completely on the help of her daughter, she has become 'her wean noo'. The indignities of incontinence and her inability to chew are encapsulated in the metaphorical phrase 'ma great tent o' nappy' and the description of 'champed egg in a cup' and 'mashed tattie'.

She finds it difficult to talk to her daughter and regrets the reversal of roles. Once the carer, she is now the recipient of her daughter's care. The phrase 'the blethers ha been plucked oot o' us' suggests that she and her daughter no longer have the comfort of shared conversations and the choice of the word 'plucked' reinforces her description of herself as 'like some skinny chicken'. It suggests a degree of self-disgust at the loss of her youthful appearance and pride in her formerly 'guid smooth skin'. Her world has contracted to her room and the view from her window. Neighbours she knew have gone and others she never sees.

Her pride, however, and desire not to be a burden prevent her from voicing her frustrations to her daughter. She replies 'Aye fine' to her daughter's solicitous question but her stoical reply is belied by 'the great heaving sigh' she gives. There is a weary resignation in her words, 'Am just biding time so am ur'. In the second last verse her words have a bleak eloquence in the personification of Time held 'between / the soft bits o' ma thumbs' and 'the skeleton underneath' her night gown. The 'glaring selfish moon' seems to signify the relentless cycle of time and the harsh reality of ageing and death.

In the last verse she contemplates her own death. Her matter-of-fact question, 'how wull she feel?' and her apparently simple and direct statements suggest a complexity of emotions about her own death and how it will affect her daughter.

'Grandpa's Soup' *(Darling*, p. 216), however, is a joyful celebration of the affection between a young child and her grandfather. In this poem Jackie Kay creates the voice of a young child expressing with uninhibited delight her pleasure in her grandfather's soup-making, her enjoyment of the finished product and her affection and admiration for him.

By making the speaker a child, Kay recreates the spontaneity and directness of a child's response to her grandfather's soup-making, which reveals the strong bond between them. In contrast the grandfather's response to the child's enthusiasm is one of self-deprecation. The child's confident statement about the unmatched quality of her grandpa's soup is re-inforced by the repetition of the phrase 'the perfect size' and the repeated idea in different words that his soup is 'the best / soup in the whole world'.

The child's pleasure in playing with the sounds of words is emphasised in the connections she makes with soup – loch, hough and sea – and she revels in the metaphorical expression 'floating / like a rich island in the middle of a soup sea'. The lines from 'He knows I will grow up and pine for it' to the exclamatory question 'Oh Grandpa, Grandpa, why is your soup so glorious?' suggest that the child is taking us, the readers or listeners, into her confidence. She is revelling in her comic exaggerations which build up to a humorous climax which demonstrates her touching acceptance that her grandpa will not always be there. The final line brings the speaker back to earth when, as a sudden afterthought, she remembers the name of 'the wee soft bits'.

3. CULTURAL IDENTITY

i. African American

As a result of her experiences of racism as a child and young woman, Jackie Kay, for a time, reacted negatively to her Scottish identity until she met Audrey Lorde, the African American poet, in 1984, who told her that she 'could be proudly African *and* Scottish' and 'should embrace both' (*Red Dust Road*, p. 201).

Introduced by her adoptive father to the singing of Bessie Smith (1894–1937), the great African American jazz and blues singer known as the Empress of the Blues, she absorbed these vital elements of African American culture. Bessie Smith, who died in hospital of wounds inflicted in a car crash, expressed, in her powerful singing, the suffering and hopes of African Americans still subjected to the harsh laws of segregation in the Southern States. As one of the foremost interpreters of the songs and poetry of the enslaved people of the American South, she created many variations of the traditional twelve-bar blues whose lyrics had an earthiness and realism far removed from the sentimentality of much of the output of the commercial song-writing industry. Kay's sequence of poems – 'Even The Trees'; 'In the Pullman'; 'The Right Season'; 'The Same Note'; 'The Red Graveyard'; 'Blues' and 'Twelve Bar Bessie' – pays tribute to the emotional power of 'her raw unplugged voice' and her fighting spirit.

'The Red Graveyard' (*Darling*, p. 73) explores her early experience of hearing Bessie Smith's singing. It is a pivotal moment, an epiphany, which leaves an indelible impression on her mind. As a young child in the back garden of her home, she hears Bessie Smith's voice in 'slow motion' and describes her impression of the power of her voice 'claiming' the rooms of the house and taking her out of herself. She describes the effect on her emotions and sense of self as

36

changing 'the shape of my silence', her inner being. She repeats the question 'Why do I remember the blues?'. There is an ambiguity in the line 'Why do I remember her voice and not my own mother's?'. Has the power of Bessie Smith's voice made her forget the sound of her mother's voice or does the description of her mother's voice refer to Bessie Smith as a spiritual mother, a mother of the imagination, whose voice has multiple properties: the hardness of rock; the sound of the wind; of hailstones; the softness of cotton; the sharpness of salt; the richness of treacle; the ripeness of a peach?

She remembers her father playing a Bessie Smith record and tapping 'a shiny beat on the floor'. She quotes his words, 'that's some voice she's got', a down-to-earth colloquial West of Scotland expression of approbation and admiration. She picks up the record cover and runs her fingers over a picture of Bessie Smith's face. The phrase 'Her magnificent black face' conveys her identification with the Empress of the Blues in the predominantly white world of her childhood.

The poem begins and ends with the same chorus, a four-line verse, the first two lines of which form a rhyming couplet, echoing the verse structure of a traditional twelve-bar blues song. In the poet's imagination, the gravestones in the grave-yard where Bessie Smith was buried open in the night 'like flowers', which seems a contradiction but suggests a super-natural transformation in the natural world. The supernatural imagery continues in the line: 'There are stones that shake and weep in the heart of night'. She imagines the singer haunting her former lovers like the young woman of the ancient ballad 'The Unquiet Grave', who cannot rest in peace until her lover ceases to mourn for her. There is the suggestion that Bessie Smith's singing had a supernatural power which reawakened the dead. The chorus could be interpreted as a metaphor for the ability of the singer to move her listeners profoundly when she sang traditional blues songs which spoke of love and loss and the hardships of life both before and after the abolition of slavery.

The first and last verses form the chorus, which frames the specific memories of the poet, and the melancholy blues tone is in contrast to the poet's joyful discovery of Bessie Smith's singing – a transformative experience – and her growing awareness of, and identification with, African American culture.

Although Bessie Smith died in 1937, her grave did not have a headstone until 1971, but the legacy of her powerful voice, the focused intensity of her singing and the inventive interpretations of the blues have lived on and inspired many of her successors.

Bessie Smith took her travelling tent shows to the people who worked the tobacco and cotton fields, hard labour for little pay or recognition. She would hold concerts in small towns where people would flock to see and hear her. Often there would be intimidation and violence from racists. **'The Right Season'** (*Darling*, pp. 71–72) opens with a verse refrain which establishes the cyclical nature of their work and the importance of the music of the blues to them as economically and politically oppressed African Americans. For them Bessie Smith was the Empress, the Voodoo Queen, whose singing and regal presence aroused deep emotions and cultural memories. This poem evokes that power.

The second verse begins with the line 'Call it a blues trail', the conversational tone continuing in the third line, 'On she would come', suggesting the commentary of a member of the audience describing the experience to a listener who was not present at the concert. The simile 'people packed in like rice in a bowl' effectively describes the crowded tent and provides proof of Bessie Smith's ability to draw in a crowd. The choice of the word 'trail' is significant. It is more usually associated with the migrations of the pioneers who opened up the plains and routes to the West Coast of America, for example the Oregon Trail. In this context, however, the poet applies the phrase to the people who travelled to the Empress's concerts. There is the sense of a pilgrimage. The alliterative sentence 'Blast the blues into them' conveys the sheer force of her singing which aroused memories of the suffering and injustice inflicted upon their families before and after the abolition of slavery. She spoke of their roots through the music of the blues.

The third verse describes the deep emotional impact of her singing. The lyrics of her songs not only evoked their suffering but also held out hope of a comforter who would lift them from 'the sad place', 'the mean place'. There was both anger and solace in her songs.

The following verse describes Bessie Smith's stage persona. The conversational opening sentence, 'And she took them', reminds us that the speaker is recounting first-hand experience. Her 'extraordinary costumes', feathers, a wig and a 'lampshade fringe' created a spectacle. The speaker, however, quickly returns to a description of her singing.

The final verse evokes memories of the 'underground railroad', a whole network of people who helped slaves escape to the Northern States before the Civil War (1861–65) between the Northern Union and the Southern Confederacy by providing safe houses and contacts. The compression of the short phrases 'Where to meet. Which house was safe. Which church' suggests the urgency and constant danger of the flight from slavery. The alliterative final line of the verse demonstrates how integral the music of the blues was to the historical and cultural experience of African Americans.

The final line of the poem echoes the first two lines, emphasising the profound connection Bessie Smith had with the people who came from the cotton and tobacco fields to hear her sing.

At many of her concerts in the travelling tent, Bessie Smith was subjected to intimidation and violence by racists but she refused to be daunted fighting back with strong words and the force of her personality. In **'Twelve Bar Bessie'**, (*Darling*, p. 75), the poet imagines an incident at one of her shows narrated by a member of the audience. She imagines the speaker urgently addressing her listeners: 'See that day, Lord, did you hear what happened then.' She has a story to tell of members of the Ku Klux Klan invading the tent where the Queen was about to sing. The phrase 'in the thick heavy air' suggests the hot, humid atmosphere of a summer night where the threat of violence is always present.

The second verse dramatically describes, in a series of phrases, the Klan members' violent intent. The speaker tells us that the Empress's stage team ran away and left her to face the masked, white-robed men alone. In verse four she is described confronting her attackers with curses and the sheer force of her personality. The speaker quotes Bessie Smith's words as hands on hips she hollers 'I'll get the whole damn lot of you out of here now'. She witheringly orders them to 'pick up the sheets and run', reducing their white robes to what they were – common bedsheets masquerading as uniforms.

The following verse vividly expresses the speaker's admiration, commenting 'That's what she done' and dramatically repeating 'You should have seen them', the colloquial expressions reflecting the fighting spirit of the Empress. The metaphor 'her voice was cast-iron' conveys not just the strength of her resolve but her unyielding, commanding presence which caused the members of the Ku Klux Klan to turn tail and flee the tent. The speaker shows her contempt for the masked, robed men whose uniform was simply sheets from someone's bed and who flew from the tent like strange birds with wings flapping to the sound of a blues song and the clapping of the black audience.

As a postscript the speaker ends her account with the words of the Empress, 'And as for you', addressed to those who stood by and did nothing. Bessie Smith's words encapsulate the speaker's admiration for the singer's fortitude, gallows humour and fighting spirit.

ii. Nigerian

In the chapter entitled 'Fantasy Africa' in her memoir *Red Dust Road* (pp. 37–48), the poet describes her childhood perceptions of Africa, formed from the assumptions of a predominantly white society which saw black people 'in a rather unsophisticated way' who were not 'afforded the right to be seen as a whole person'. Africa was seen as a 'whole mass', not individual countries with diverse languages and cultures: the dark continent 'civilised' by Christianity and colonial rule. As she was growing up, Kay became aware that this narrative still prevailed in much of British society and contributed to a feeling of alienation so that, as she says, 'part of me was foreign and strange to myself'.

A number of years before Kay had traced her father and she was travelling from London to Manchester by train, a black man sitting opposite her looked her in the face and said suddenly 'I bet you are an Ibo – definitely'. She described it as such a striking experience that she wrote the poem **'Pride'** (*Darling*, pp. 160–62).

The Ibo people are one of the largest ethnic groups in Africa. They live mainly in the south-eastern part of Nigeria, one of the most densely populated regions in the whole of the African continent. Their language, Ibo, has many dialects and a standardised written form has been in use since 1962. English is often preferred as it is seen as the language of status and opportunity. The main religion of the region is Christianity which co-exists with ancient Ibo religious beliefs practised in

traditional rites of passage. Their culture emphasises respect
for the elderly and values education. The region is agricul-
turally rich, growing yam, cassava and taro, and it harvests
palm oil as a cash crop. Ibo people are predominantly traders,
farmers, fishermen and craftsmen but their communities have
experienced migration from the early days of the slave trade
to the present day. Ibo culture is rich in visual art, music and
dance forms. The masquerade, for example, is a traditional
feature of harvest celebrations when participants wear masks
to resemble the spirits of the dead. Paul Robeson, the great
singer, Chinua Achebe, the author of the seminal novel *Things
Fall Apart*, Chimamanda Ngozi Adichie, the author of *Half
of a Yellow Sun*, a novel of modern Nigeria, much of which is
set during the Biafran War in the years 1967 to 1970, and
many others are Ibos. It is this ancient rich culture which the
poet experiences when she travels to Nigeria in 2003 and 2009.

Although **'Pride'** is based on the poet's actual experience,
this narrative poem is much more than a naturalistic account
of her encounter with the black man on the train. The poet's
imagination transforms this actual episode into a fable which
illustrates the complex nature of identity: the pride a sense
of belonging to a particular group engenders, but also the
danger of exceptionalism, the 'wha's like us' attitude which
can lead to a sense of superiority and racism.

The poet treats these themes with a light touch. The poem
is a cautionary tale told with humour, ending with an affirmative flourish of the imagination. The poet imagines the welcome
she would receive when she visited her ancestral village. It is
an idealised vision of her ancestral home and indicates a deep
need to discover a vital missing part of her identity – her
Nigerian roots. She has her father's genes but at this stage of
her life does not know him or his culture.

In the opening verse the poet describes the intense gaze of
a black man sitting opposite her which suggests more than a

passing connection between them, commenting that it was 'as if he and I went a long way back'. So penetrating is his gaze that the poet uses hyperbole to describe his effect on her: 'My whole childhood, I'm quite sure / passed before him'. She imagines him as a little boy in Africa 'on a red dust road'. The words 'and then he spoke' signal a dramatic opening to their conversation: '"Ibo," he said, "Ibo, definitely."' The sense of drama at this revelation is maintained in the poet's account of what happened next. He thumped the table, her 'coffee jumped and spilled', people were roused from sleep and the night train sped noisily through the dark English countryside.

The following verse reinforces the humorous exaggeration, the poet commenting ironically that she 'had no doubt, from the way he said it, / that Ibo noses are the best noses in the world' and comes to a humorous climax in the last four lines of the verse in which the poet states that her face had become a map and the stranger had located her ancestral village in Nigeria in the lower part of her jaw.

The following two verses continue the conceit, the stranger telling the poet the meaning of her father's name and 'transforming' into her brother, her father as a young man or any member of her large clan. She asks him to tell her about the Ibo people and he responds with the same look of pride in his clan that she had seen on the faces of Scottish clan members: 'a MacLachlan, a MacDonnell, a MacLeod': a pride in their origins and a certainty about who they were. To her repeated plea 'Tell me about the Ibos', the stranger praises the qualities of the Ibos who are 'clever, reliable, / dependable, faithful, true'. Her next question 'And what, I asked, are the Ibos faults?' elicits the unconditional reply 'Faults? No faults. Not a single one'.

In the final verse she imagines the welcome she would receive when she visited her ancestral village. It is an idealised picture, created by the stranger, of her reception by the whole village: there would be 'Massive celebrations. Definitely'. She responds to his enthusiasm picturing her arrival in the village and her meeting with her grandparents. She begins to dance and words and phrases of the Ibo language fall from her mouth 'like seeds'. Although idealised, her vision of her welcome is genuinely felt and reveals her strong need to find her African roots.

In her memoir, Jackie Kay gives a detailed account of her search for her birth father, Jonathan. She knew he had studied Agriculture and Forestry at the University of Aberdeen and could therefore be traced by his name and profession. On putting his name into Google, she very quickly found him. The entry had a photograph of him and an article about his specialised work on trees. It also had a phone number and the poet decided to phone him immediately. They speak for the first time and in the course of their conversation he tells her that, as well as his professional work as a tree specialist, he has become a born-again Christian and practises as a lay reader in the Anglican Church of Nigeria. He agrees to meet her when she is in Abuja for a literary event. Her account of this first and only meeting with him is both comedic and deeply painful. Her father prays for her, dances round the room, 'whirling like a dervish' in the heat of religious fervour. There is a laying on of hands and a wish that she 'be cleansed'. He considers her as his 'past sin' and for that reason tells her he must keep her existence secret from his wife, his family and his church congregation unless she agrees to accept the Lord and be born again. The poet comments that she did not 'feel angry or bitter' but rather 'spent and exhausted'. As a result of her refusal to be born again, he would not agree to any further meetings and insisted that she remained a secret. On a subsequent visit to Nigeria in 2009 she met his son Sidney who welcomed her warmly and found it hard to accept that his father would not acknowledge her. It was not the Ibo way, he told her. In their culture a father always acknowledges his child no matter the circumstances.

After her visits to Nigeria, Jackie Kay wrote a number of poems exploring the emotional impact of her meeting with her father and her experiences of the landscape and Ibo culture of south-eastern Nigeria. As a child she had imagined the African landscape as flat with rich dark earth; there was 'a red dust road'. As an adult she walked the red dust road which led to her ancestral village where she was welcomed, not by her father, but by a cousin nursing her baby. The poems are evocative, reflecting her conflicting emotions as she experienced the complex reality of her African roots.

In her poem **'Burying My African Father'** (*Fiere*, p. 29), she tells of her final acceptance of the fact that they will not meet again. The poem is addressed to Jonathan and takes us on her walk to her father's home in Nzagha. It is an evocative description of the African landscape, the 'red dust road' leading to the village of Nzagha, the animals, the plants and the fruits of this region in Nigeria. The structure of the poem beginning with 'Now' and the sequence of two-line verses beginning with 'and' takes us step by step on the poet's walk to her father's compound where she meets her cousin and holds her cousin's two-week-old baby. There is a sense of immediacy in the recounting of her quest and a warmth in her reply '*Odimma*', meaning 'Fine thank you', to her cousin's shy word of welcome '*Kedu*', meaning 'how are you?'. But her father is not there. With a sudden transition to her memory of the meeting with her father in the hotel room in Abuja, where he danced and prayed, she reminds him with poignant understatement that he would not at that meeting reveal the name of his village or the names of his children. There is a sad irony in the contrast between the friendly welcome of her cousin and the refusal of her father to meet her in his home.

The final three verses begin with an echo of the structure of the first line of the poem but, instead of the sense of a journey undertaken with hope, the 'Now' reinforces the absence of her father and her acceptance that she must end her search for him. Her words are not bitter but rather an acknowledgement that they will not meet again. There is a poignancy in the poet's words as she accepts that, although she has arrived 'to the home of the ancestors', it is without him. The final verses speak of her resolve to metaphorically 'bury' him in her imagination, the final couplet with its mono-syllabic end rhymes bringing an emotional force to the final words of the poem.

'Ukpor Market' (*Fiere*, p. 8) is a compressed statement of the complex reality of the poet's experience of Nigeria. It illustrates her need for connection with her African roots and the contrast between her perceptions of herself as a black woman and the perceptions of the women she meets in the market at Ukpor.

The poem begins with the poet's observation: 'In the market in Ukpor / I saw a row of women / with my face'. Struck by the resemblance, she describes them as her 'mirror image', the repetitive phrases beginning with the word 'same' empha-sising the poet's perception of them as very similar in appear-ance to her. The only difference she could see 'was another shade of black'. They greet her with the word '*Oyinbo*'. Eager to make contact and connection, she responds enthusiastically but does not understand the meaning of the word they use as they touch her skin admiringly. The poet thinks they are acknowledging that she is one of them, replying that 'Yes, my father / is an Igbo'. Her companion, Kachi, tells her gently what '*Oyinbo*' means. He explains that it is '*a pidgin word / for white woman*'. The poet does not directly comment on their perception of her as a white woman but allows the narrative to reveal the irony of the situation.

'Road to Amaudo' (*Fiere*, pp. 52–53) explores the theme of solidarity in the face of obstacles and hardship both physical and mental. It culminates in a plea for a shared endeavour in the constant struggle to achieve peace in the minds of individuals and in the wider community. It is effective at both a literal and metaphorical level.

The irregular lines of the poem are organised on the page to suggest a long winding road. It is prefaced by the comment that Amaudo means 'the village of peace' in Ibo and is brought to a conclusion with the Ibo words: '*ka udo di, ka ndu di*' (let there be peace, let there be life).

The first section describes the road to Amaudo as long and winding, 'a red dust road' which seems to be never ending. For the travellers bearing their heavy loads it carries the promise of things to come, a way forward and is simultaneously a link to the past. At the beginning of the second section, the phrase 'the road to Amaudo' is repeated. It suggests that it has carried the feet of many over centuries. The poet states that it 'is at times impassable: / but pass people do', suggesting a determination to find a way forward against the odds. The choice of the word 'hefting' in the phrase 'hefting the load' signifies literally the sheer physical effort of carrying a heavy load on their backs and metaphorically their hopes of a better life and for peace. The phrase 'the frail weight of peace' seems at first contradictory, but it emphasises that a state of peace is vulnerable; that it can easily be shattered by forces beyond their control. The repetitive phrases 'round one corner / [...] round one bend, then the next' reinforces the impression of the long exhausting journeys undertaken by whole families seeking perhaps safety or a better life. The physical features of this road – the elephant grasses and the deep red soil – place them in a familiar landscape. Personified as 'a constant companion, / a compadre, a fiere', the road has seen journeys undertaken by generation upon generation from time immemorial.

The final section begins with an invitation, 'Come let us go / down the road to Amaudo', an invitation almost like a chant to join the men, women and children in solidarity with them. The lines 'and shake hands / with our old selves' could be interpreted as both a renewal of their connections with their ancestors and of their own psychological healing. There is the suggestion that many have been 'lost to their families / or lost to themselves'. The poet identifies with them and invites us to do likewise. The phrase *'those* people; *you, me'* – changing from the impersonal, often pejorative 'those people' to the individual 'you, me' – encapsulates the profound change in attitude to mental suffering required by all of us before inner peace can be achieved. It is an inclusive vision of mental healing. The poet ends with the affirmative statement: 'I want to walk on the road to Amaudo'. It is a gesture of solidarity, of the sharing of the trials and tribulations of life with her fellow travellers. She is their 'compadre', their 'fiere'. The poem ends with a reference to the road she had literally walked down to enter Nzagha, her ancestral village. For the poet seeking her African roots, it is a symbolic physical and psychological journey.

iii. Scottish

Jackie Kay felt that an essential element of her role as Scotland's Makar (national poet) was to stimulate a 'national conversation'. **'Threshold'** (*Bantam*, pp. 15–20) was written to commemorate the opening session of the Scottish Parliament in 2016. It is a warm, spirited invitation to the members of parliament and all the people of Scotland to respect and cherish democracy in an inclusive society regardless of a person's ethnicity or status. It calls for the people of Scotland to celebrate the diverse cultures and languages of a multi-racial country. There is no room for exceptionalism, the 'wha's like us' mentality. It is written with panache and humour.

In the first section, the poet issues an invitation to all of us, not in the lofty rhetoric of traditional ceremonial occasions but in colloquial Scots, 'Let's hae a blether about doors', using the extended metaphor of the many kinds of doors whose thresholds we must pass over in the course of our lives. It is important to remember that, historically, the marking of a door was to signal persecution or plague and at the end of this section the poet emphasises the importance of remembering our past: of opening a door on the knowledge of the injustices of the Highland Clearances; of the skills of the men who built the great ships of the Clyde; of Donald Dewar, the politician who was instrumental in the establishing of the Scottish Parliament: 'Take the big key and open the door to the breathing past / [...] Then picture yourself on the threshold, / The exact moment when you might begin again'. Directly addressing her audience, the poet is calling for new beginnings in political and civic Scotland.

The second section extends the invitation, 'Come through to this Parliament, new session!', which must represent the many communities and landscapes of Scotland – the towns and cities, the lochs and glens, the Highlands and Islands – as an integral part of the infinite variety of the universe: 'the hail clanjamfrie' (the phrase which concludes Hugh MacDiarmid's poem 'The Bonnie Broukit Bairn'). The poet offers strong advice: 'Find here what you are looking for: / Democracy: guard her // Like you would a small daughter'. The imperative verbs and the comparison emphasise the importance of the message: that democracy is precious and vulnerable and must be protected and nurtured. Continuing the doors metaphor, Kay emphasises that Scotland should welcome the world's refugees and all its new citizens in all their diversity of cultures and talents. They are as much a part of the country as William Wallace, the poets, the fisherwoman from Jura or Arthur Wharton, Scotland's first black professional footballer. This section ends with the stirring words: 'Our strength is our difference. / Dinny fear it. Dinny caw canny.'

In the final section, Kay quotes words of welcome in many of the world's languages. Her emphasis is on the importance of diversity, 'It takes more than one language to tell a story', repeating the statement in colloquial Scots: 'Wan patter is naer enough'. She brings the address to a conclusion as she began – with a friendly invitation: 'C'mon ben the hoose. / Come join our brilliant gathering.' It is a timely message that the Parliament is not a remote legislature but a democratic forum in which all the citizens of Scotland have a voice.

The importance of language as a fundamental part of an individual's sense of self and cultural identity is illustrated in the poem **'Old Tongue'** (*Darling*, pp. 190–91). It portrays the process of assimilation into a new culture and the effect this experience has on a young child's language. The speaker tells us that when she was eight years old, she was 'forced south', the phrase clearly indicating that she had not wanted to leave her childhood home. She expresses a degree of surprise that she has lost her Scottish accent and no longer uses words which had been second nature to her. They had fallen off her tongue, not in the sense of using the Scots expressions natural to her but in the sense of a falling off, of a loss of her Scots language. She lists the words and expressions she misses: expressive words such as *dreich, wabbit* and *crabbit* and colloquial phrases used by squabbling children such as *shut yer geggie* and *I'll gie you the malkie.*

In colourful imagery she describes how her pronunciation changed as she was growing up: 'My own vowels started to stretch like my bones'. She confesses that she had rejected her Scottish tongue, forgetting words and expressions and adopting new English words. The metaphor 'marched in' has connotations of an army taking over. She cites examples of stretched vowels in words such as 'ghastly, awful, / quite dreadful', which she feels do not have the colloquial vigour of her old words. She humorously voices her mock indignation when 'scones' is pronounced like 'stones' and 'pokey hats' become 'ice cream cones'. She continues in humorous vein, 'Oh where did all my words go – / my old words, my lost words?', and dramatically builds her lament to a climax, exclaiming that she would have swallowed her 'wandering' words rather than lose them.

In the final verse she continues her personification of her 'old words', which 'buried themselves' in 'the English soil', exclaiming 'I wanted them back; I wanted my old accent back, / my old tongue'. In the last two lines she reverts to using Scots words such as 'dour' and 'soor'. She describes her old tongue in the alliterative phrase 'Sing-songy', which suggests the cadences of her Scots speech. Her final words are a spirited humorous affirmation of her love of her Scots tongue: 'I wanted to *gie it laldie*.'

By means of humour and a child's self-dramatisation, the poet is making the point that early language loss can damage a child's sense of self and confidence in her native culture. Adoption of another language or dialect should not cancel out one's native tongue. There is room for both. As the poet states in 'Threshold', 'Wan patter is naer enough'; 'It takes more than one language to tell a story'.

In **'Watching People Sing'** (*Darling*, pp. 76–77), Jackie Kay recreates her experience of party socials as she was growing up, where communal and individual singing brought people together in conviviality. Such occasions were a feature of a particular Scottish culture which combined political activism with a love of song and storytelling. She did not participate in the singing but was keenly aware of the power of singing to bring people out of themselves and to move them deeply. She captures the fun and uninhibited pleasure of these occasions with humour and affection.

She names individuals describing their choice of song, their singing styles and banter with vivid imagery and colloquial expressions: 'When Alec sings *Ae Fond Kiss* / his soft lips part like petals'; 'Peter's chin, doing its dinger, / judders, hings on to the last note'. A reluctant guest is coaxed to sing. The poet's father sings traditional and music hall songs with panache. The house reverberates to the singing and voices of people enjoying a shared pleasure.

In the final three verses the poet moves from a description of the occasion to the reflections of her older self: 'People are what they've been in this room. / A good dancer. A patter merchant. *What a night, eh?*' For a moment in time they have recaptured their younger selves. At sixteen, the poet had felt she was 'too old' for the uninhibited conviviality and nostalgia of the evening and 'Yet still,' she remarks, 'Anna's voice / singing *John Anderson my Jo John*' moves her deeply. This tender, poignant song of enduring love, written by Robert Burns, brings her sixteen-year-old self to the sudden realisation of the inevitability of death and the need for comfort and love at the end of life. It is a fitting tribute to the people who nourished her own cultural awakening and creativity.

'The Ardtornish Quartet' (*Bantam*, pp. 37–42) is a series of poems which describe the landscape and communities of a remote area of the West Highlands. The poet's visit to Rose Cottage on the Ardtornish Estate evokes memories and heightens her sense of the passing of time. The poems are reflective but not sombre and emphasise the importance of community in an area where the landscape and climate can make daily living challenging.

The first poem, **'Rose Cottage'**, illustrates a coincidence. Standing outside Rose Cottage in Ardtornish years after her birth and adoption, the poet imagines her birth mother in the Rose Cottage in Nairn, where she lived as a girl and young woman, in a troubled sleep during her pregnancy. She describes her as 'heart heavy' but finding 'Solace in the spill of yellow fields' in the morning light. Years after her mother had given birth, she is spending time in another Rose Cottage on the Ardtornish Estate in Morvern, Argyll. At night, she shines a torch to watch 'the river / Rush as if to meet a lover, dark as the past'. There is perhaps an allusion to the lover, her Nigerian birth father. In the morning she finds comfort in the 'river running still', a symbol of the passing of time but also of an enduring natural presence.

In contrast, the second poem, **'Lochaline Stores'**, is an affectionate, humorous tribute to the local shop in Lochaline, the main village of the Morvern district. It illustrates the essential role the store has in the small communities of this remote area.

It begins with the emphatic statement, 'Nothing can be hidden from Lochaline Stores'. Then, in a series of humorous, self-deprecatory repetitive phrases, it lists the many and various needs of the poet herself and its customers. It knows in detail the habits and foibles of its customers, but the poet does not see this knowledge in a negative light and rather considers the social interaction essential to the life and well-being of the community. The poet emphasises this social function telling herself not to get upset by its knowledge of her own and its customers' lives with a degree of humorous hyperbole, advising that it knows 'your innermost thoughts'; it is 'the empathetic store'. Using the pronouns 'you' and 'yours' inclusively, she addresses herself, the customers of the store and us, the readers, inviting us to share her experience. The humorous admonition is reinforced by the reference to the phrase 'retail therapy' and the use of the end rhymes 'psychoanalysis' and 'paralysis'. This section of the poem ends on a more serious note. People come to the store for 'something more' than essential supplies. They are looking for 'A small bit talk for the short days, long nights'.

The final verse is an evocative description of 'the windy drive back' to the cottage on the single-track road through an iconic West Highland landscape of pine trees, cattle grids, passing places, deer and sheep. The journey marks the transition from the comfort and social interaction the store provides to the darkness of a potentially hazardous drive to the poet's holiday home.

'Ardtornish Dark' is an atmospheric poem which contrasts the lights of the village of Lochaline and the headlights of occasional passing cars and the light left on in the poet's holiday cottage in anticipation of her return with the growing darkness of the night, and the social contact of the village community with the isolation of her cottage.

The poet uses the image of a 'slow ballet dancer's last pirouette' to describe the gradual fading of the light 'Across the dark waters of Loch Aline'. The small lights of the village flutter; car headlights 'flicker' and 'suddenly shimmer' and there is a 'glimmer' of sunset from the opposite shore of the loch. These evocative words emphasise the contrast between light and darkness. The poet describes walking past 'fish-nets bundled like lost souls', the simile creating a ghostly atmosphere in which everyday objects take on a mysterious aspect as the day fades into the darkness of night.

On her return to the cottage, she is alone and banishes any feeling of loneliness reminding herself to light the fire and dance around the room to the song *'Come on baby light my fire'*. Significantly, she also uses the expression 'light your own fire' metaphorically, suggesting with humour a determination to enjoy her independence and find pleasure in her own company. In this atmospheric poem, the poet vividly conveys her experience of this area of the West Highlands.

'**Croft Near Croig**' is a poem of memories in which the poet quietly celebrates her childhood experiences of holidays on a croft near Croig on the island of Mull. Geographically, Mull is closely linked by a ferry from Lochaline and these two connected areas of the West Highlands have played and continue to play an important part in the poet's life.

The poem opens with the observation that 'What each of us holds dear is a mystery'. Nostalgia cannot easily be explained. The poet, remembering family holidays on a croft near Croig, a small community on the island of Mull, feels nostalgia for the pleasure of eating slabs of cheddar; for the sharing of legends and stories; the viewing of an 'iconic ruin'. Returning to Croig many years later, she finds the croft house has a new roof and its interior has been renovated. The original stone walls, however, are still intact and she has no difficulty in picturing herself as a young girl 'Putting on a show, dancing', her brother watching from 'the gods', the theatrical reference suggesting he is perched precariously above her. Her memory of her parents relaxed in holiday mood, enjoying the view from the roof, is still fresh in her mind, 'unchanged, lifting the heart, now as then'.

The use of 'we' suggests her visit was with her parents. They share memories of the people they knew and the late-night ceilidhs. The sense of belonging, if only for a short time, to a welcoming community is a fundamental element of their West Highland holidays.

The final verse evokes the various sensory experiences the poet particularly remembers: the taste of milk straight from the goat, the scents of ferns and bracken and the beauty of Calgary Bay with its pristine white sands. Such memories are precious.

Descriptive and reflective, the poems of 'The Ardtornish Quartet' invite us to share in the poet's experiences of a beautiful part of Scotland and express her affection for

the people and landscapes of this remote area of the West
Highlands.

'Maw Broon Visits a Therapist' (*Darling*, pp. 150–51) is one
of several poems featuring the archetypal Scottish matriarch
in the comic strip 'The Broons', created by writer and editor
R. D. Low and artist Dudley D. Watkins and first published
in the *Sunday Post* in 1936. It continues to be published weekly
and over the years the strip has been modified and updated by
various writers and artists. It remains true, however, to the
original concept of a humorous, affectionate portrayal of the
ups and downs of a large working-class family living together
in a small tenement flat in a Scottish city or town. They speak
in a mixture of Scots and English using exclamatory words
such as 'Crivvens', 'Jings' and 'Help ma boab', not commonly
used in everyday modern Scots.

In the strip, Maw Broon is depicted as the capable, dependable matriarch, managing Paw Broon and her large family of
eight. In her poems, however, Jackie Kay puts her into alien
situations in which she struggles with aspects of the modern
world. Using the dramatic monologue form, the poet has great
fun imagining Maw Broon in a session with a psychotherapist
and portrays her finding her voice and briefly stepping out of
her box to assert herself as more than the self-sacrificing,
trauchled housewife.

The first four stanzas reveal that she feels she cannot
cope anymore and cannot express what she feels. She admits
that she 'canny hawnle life' anymore; that she has 'aye worn /
this same pinnie and this heid scarf'. She is in a rut. The
following verses develop her conversation with the therapist,
expressing with anxious irritation her inability to open up
and talk about herself. She questions the stock technique of
analysing dreams and complains that this therapy is making
her 'crabbit'. When the therapist asks her how she sees herself,
she begins to reveal more explicitly her dissatisfaction with

herself and in doing so finds she can express herself with fluency and vivid comic imagery. She is 'fed up' with her bun which she describes as 'a big onion / at the back o' ma heid'. She plays on both the literal and metaphorical meanings of the expression 'A' canny let ma hair doon'. She says she is 'built like a bothy', mirroring her image in the comic strip. She relishes using the alliterative phrase 'wabbit and crabbit'. Suddenly realising that in fact she can 'see' herself, she pauses dramatically and says 'Here – A'm quite guid / at this therapy lark eh?' and challenges the therapist: 'Here, Maw Broon could be a therapist. / [...] Jings, it's money for auld rope', expressing her scepticism about the efficacy of the therapist's treatment in a less than tactful manner. Maw Broon has found her voice and is expressing what she really feels.

In the penultimate verse she expands the meaning of the phrase 'auld rope', using it as a simile to express her main complaint: that of being taken for granted, of always being the one to do whatever is demanded of her. Her last words are ambiguous. She finds her new-found freedom to speak her mind 'exciting' but is equally aware that such a change is unsettling. It is as if she will once again be confined to her box, the stereotypical Scottish matriarch of her motley brood.

It is perhaps an error to read too much into Jackie Kay's humorous take on one of the characters of 'The Broons', but underlying the fun there is an insightful appreciation of the popular culture which made Maw Broon such an iconic figure who, though trapped in a particular time and place while the world moves on, lives on in our imaginations.

4. IDENTITY DENIED

i. Racism and Slavery

'In my country' (*Darling*, p. 82) is an intensely felt poem arising from Jackie Kay's experience of racial prejudice. As a child and young woman, she was frequently questioned about where she came from and was subjected to cruel racial abuse. The poem expresses an unpalatable, universal truth about the darker aspects of human nature: the age-old fear of the stranger who is not of the tribe, and the urge to attack or ostracise anyone who is of a different colour, culture or creed.

The speaker describes meeting a woman who, on seeing the colour of her skin, treats her with suspicion and mistrust. Using imagery which does not signify a specific time or place, the poet takes this encounter into an almost mythical realm, detached from a specific time and place, in order to demonstrate the primitive fear of the other, which continues to blight the lives of individuals and particular communities.

The first three lines describe the speaker walking at the mouth of a river. The personification of the 'honest river' which 'shakes hands with the sea' suggests a natural harmony with which the speaker identifies. It is brutally shattered by the behaviour of the woman who walks round her like an animal circling its prey or witch-hunters choosing their victim. The phrase 'as if I were a superstition' dehumanises the speaker, reflecting the woman's own superstitious, irrational prejudice towards anyone not of her tribe. She can only see a stereotype not an individual human being.

The poet uses the paragraph break for dramatic effect, emphasising the speaker's intense hurt and anger at the woman's behaviour in the forceful metaphor 'or the worst dregs of her imagination'. The colloquial directness of the following line 'so when she finally spoke' further intensifies the hurt the speaker feels. The woman not only circles round her but subjects her to silent, hostile scrutiny. By slowly emphasising each word of the question *'Where do you come from?'*, the woman reveals her deep-rooted prejudice and ignorance. The metaphor 'her words spliced into bars / of an old wheel' suggests that this question has been repeated over and over again from century to century in a constant cycle of prejudice. By replying that she also comes from 'Here. These parts', the speaker proudly and defiantly asserts her identity and challenges that prejudice. It is a fitting climax to the poem.

ii. *The Lamplighter*

Introduction

Jackie Kay was asked to write a work for radio by BBC radio producer Pam Fraser Solomon to mark the two hundredth anniversary in 2007 of the Abolition of the Slave Trade. Initially reluctant to do so but, in her own words, 'realising that many of the inequalities and divisions in our society today were the result of the slave trade', she felt morally bound to write about it.

Having undertaken detailed research into original accounts and histories of the slave trade, she used these 'shocking original testimonies' and historical analyses to create her radio play ***The Lamplighter***. She writes in her introduction to the 2020 edition of the play that 'Too much information about the actual experience of it fills most ordinary people, black and white, with revulsion, distaste, or worse, induces boredom', but she felt compelled to recreate in detail the lives of individual women forced into slavery and document the historical facts of the British slave trade. She does not spare Scotland nor the city of Glasgow for a reluctance to acknowledge their participation in the slave trade and calls for the country not only to acknowledge its shameful role in the trade but also to be educated in 'the history of the plantations alongside the history of the Highland Clearances'. In her final remarks, she emphasises that the history of the slave trade is not 'black history'. It is world history. It concerns us all.

Non-naturalistic in style, the play has been described as a 'tragic choral poem'. It focuses on the lives of four women: Lamplighter, Black Harriot, Constance and Mary. Taken by kidnappers from their West African villages, they endured the horrors of the Atlantic passage on slave ships, the brutalities of the slave markets in British port cities and transportation to the sugar plantations of the West Indies to labour as field hands in the cane fields until finally they achieved their freedom. As the play progresses, they tell not only their own individual, distinctive stories but also voice the historical facts of the slave trade over several hundred years. They were robbed of their identity, their childhood and youth; sexually assaulted and forced into early motherhood; separated from their children and whipped and beaten: experiences common to them all. They speak for the generations of Africans sold into slavery, bearing witness to the brutality and horror of the slave trade over several centuries and holding British complicity in it to account. The only male character, MacBean, is a composite figure who represents at different points in the play a slave ship's captain, a slave trader, a plantation owner, a chronicler of slave-trade legislation and, latterly, of the parliamentary legislation which abolished the slave trade.

Structure

The play has sixteen scenes which encompass the history of the British slave trade from the seventeenth to the nineteenth century. Within this broad narrative, Jackie Kay recreates the lives of four individual African women forced into slavery. Although their accounts are broadly chronological, the women visit and revisit their experiences in the course of the play. The intermingling of their voices is choral in effect. The playwright's directions at the beginning of Scene 4 clearly state that 'The same chorus of three women will accompany the telling of the Lamplighter's story, to give the impression that any single story is a multiple one' (p. 7). They call and respond to one another, enabling the listener or reader to imagine them as distinctive individuals in the repeated act of remembering the trauma of their suffering rather than anonymous slaves on a slave ship register. Throughout the play, when Lamplighter voices particular aspects of her story, each woman takes up her words, adding to them in her own reiteration of the theme. In Scene 4, for example, Lamplighter speaks of her enslavement:

> LAMPLIGHTER   I am jumbled with the span of years, and the
> weight of things.
> The weight of a horse bit in my mouth.
> BLACK HARRIOT   The weight of a chain on my arm.
> MARY   The weight of my body
> On the scales before I was sold.
> CONSTANCE   The weight of my heavy heart.   (p. 11)

In the recurring scenes entitled 'Shipping News', the repeated recitation of the shipping forecasts, the descriptions of the Atlantic storms and the documenting of the deaths of anonymous slaves in a ship's register reinforce the relentless cyclical nature of the slave trade:

> The *Annapolis* reached London –
> Less than a third of the slaves survived.
> Captain's Log: 23rd May 1709 –
> Buryed a man slave No 84.
> Wednesday 29 May –
> Buryed a Boy slave, No 86 of a flux.
> Decreasing. Rough or very rough.   (p. 4)

Lamplighter is the leading character whose story provides a framework for the stories of the other three women. As herself as the young girl Anniwaa, she speaks virtually the same opening and closing words of the play: 'Once upon a time, I lived in a house with a cone-shaped roof in a big compound. My mother grew okra and pumpkin in her yard. My father shaped woods and metals.'

Sound

As a purely aural medium, the play uses different voices speaking individually or in chorus, deploys many varied sound effects to evoke particular locations and includes spirituals, hymns, lullabies and traditional popular songs. In Scene 1, for example, the sounds are of '*the sea slapping against the walls of Cape Coast Castle. The sound of many different African languages, talking fast, scared*' (p. 1). At the beginning of Scene 11, entitled 'Runaway', the directions state: '*We hear the sound of running and bush being cut and the ominous beating of a drum. The barking of dogs. The firing of a gun*' (p. 53). Communal singing of spirituals brings comfort to the women giving them strength to endure and a hope, against all the odds, that they will one day be free. In Scene 8, the women speak of their lives of hard labour in the sugar cane fields. Together and then individually they sing the words of the spiritual 'Go down Moses'. It voices the cries of the Old Testament Israelites, enslaved by the Pharaoh in Egypt, and has a tragic resonance for them:

ALL   *Go down, Moses, way down in Egypt's land*
            Tell old Pharaoh, Let my people go.
BLACK HARRIOT   *Go down Moses*
MARY   *way down Egypt's land*
CONSTANCE   *Tell old Pharaoh,*
ALL   *Let my people go.*   (p. 43)

Their renditions of their own parodies of popular songs – for example, 'I Belong to Glasgow' (p. 66) and 'Money Makes the World Go Round' (p. 68) – provide an ironic commentary on the trade in sugar, tobacco and cotton which made so many British merchants rich and drove the exponential growth of British port cities.

Characters: The Women's Voices

1. Lamplighter

In Scene 1, Anniwaa, a young girl of eleven, begins her story: 'Once upon a time, I lived in a house with a cone-shaped roof, in a big compound. My mother grew okra and pumpkin in her yard. My father shaped wood and metals.' (p. 1).

Having been kidnapped by slavers, she is speaking from the West African fort, Cape Coast Castle, which is a holding prison for slaves who will be transported to Britain and then taken to the sugar plantations of the West Indies. Separated from her brother, she endures the brutal confinement of the fort where she is 'trapped and kept like an animal' (p. 2). She hears sounds she has never heard before: 'They say it is The Sea. I think it is a wild monster. I think it is coming for me.' (p. 2). She becomes more and more malnourished and fears she will never leave the fort's dungeon alive.

In Scene 4, Anniwaa, as a mature woman renamed 'Lamplighter' who has written down her story, addresses the reader:

> Reader, be assured this narrative is no fiction.
> I have not written my experiences in order to attract attention to myself. On the contrary, my description falls far short of the facts. It is not my intention to horrify.
> [...]
> Nobody ever told my story before.

I was the one who was recaptured and sold
For eighty pounds, on December 8th 1792,
forced then to board a vessel at Lamplighter's Hall,
Avonmouth, heading for the plantations.   (p. 7)

Transported on the *Mary* she endured wild Atlantic storms and appalling conditions and, against all the odds, survived to tell her story. The act of remembering her experiences is a deeply painful one but, once freed from slavery, she felt compelled to tell her story:

I can still stretch my arms back and be able to touch it again,
smell it again, taste it again. Slavery.   (p. 12)

In Scene 6, Lamplighter remembers her life before enslavement when she and her brother belonged to the entire village. As she toils in the cane fields, she remembers her happy childhood but it seemed to her that it was another girl who 'lived that blessed life'. She likes to think:

she is up there, still,
mysterious, magical girl,
that she would never ever
hear this story.   (p. 16)

Taken from back-breaking work in the sugar cane fields, Lamplighter became a kitchen hand in the plantation owner's house. The work was equally exhausting and debilitating. There was no respite from the drudgery. The owner's wife, referred to as The HouseLady, tried to teach her 'the precepts of God's word. Thou shalt love thy neighbour as thyself', completely unaware of the bitter irony of teaching Christian love to her slave. Lamplighter comments: 'I suppose she never saw me as her neighbour' (p. 23).

Forced to board a vessel heading for the plantations at Lamplighter's Hall, Avonmouth, Anniwaa was renamed Lamplighter. She alludes to 'that constant flame' of hope which would not be extinguished, despite the terrible hardships she endured, and her slave name takes on a symbolic resonance: 'They call me the Lamplighter' (p. 35).

In Scene 8, entitled 'Sugar', Lamplighter describes her work as a field hand on a plantation in Jamaica: 'planting, cutting, burning, carrying, loading, slicing and stripping' the sugar cane (p. 39) in preparation for processing in the sugar mill in order to satisfy the British demand for sugar, to satisfy the British sweet tooth. When she ran away dogs were sent after her and, once she had been caught, her master flogged her. Taken from the field work, she served as the slave owner's cook for many years, subjected to repeated whippings until her 'back was all corruption' (p. 43).

In Scene 10, entitled 'Death – free at last', Lamplighter speaks of the deadly diseases which the slaves on the plantations succumbed to:

> When one of us died
> Of leprosy, TB, pneumonia or yellow fever
> [...]
> We couldn't take no more
> Out in the sugar fields   (p. 49)

She describes the hurried burial, repeating the words: 'No time now, no time to mourn the dead' and cries out 'Free at last! Free at last!' (p. 50). With the other women she repeats the names of fellow slaves who have died a sugar death – Clarissa, Phoebe, Raveface, Sally, Mountain Lucy – and whose only memorials are in the memories of those who have survived.

In Scene 11, entitled 'Runaway', all the women tell of the many slaves who ran away and of the Slave Codes of many of the islands of the West Indies. Lamplighter tells us that she ran away five times:

> Four times they got me and brought me back.
> Even the forty lashes on my back,
> Even the hundred and forty,
> Didn't stop me trying again.   (p. 57)

On the fifth time she ran away, she succeeded in evading recapture and survived to tell her story. She remembers that when her owner told her that she must obey his every command and surrender to his will, 'never before had my puny arm felt so strong' (p. 59) and she vowed that one day she would be free.

In Scene 12, Lamplighter describes her experience of the slave ships crossing the Atlantic:

> Nothing to see but sea
> Nothing to hear but roar
> Nothing to smell but blood and gore
> Nothing to taste but salt and rice
> Nothing to sense but fear.   (p. 60)

She states that she would rather die on the gallows than live in slavery.

In the following scene, entitled 'British Cities', Lamplighter highlights Britain's role in the slave trade which led to the rapid growth and prosperity of the cities of London, Birmingham, Manchester, Liverpool, Bristol, Glasgow, Edinburgh, Lancaster and Hull. She asserts 'I put those cities on the map' (p. 64). She had contributed, along with thousands of other slaves, to the trade in sugar, tobacco and cotton which had stimulated the development of Britain as a powerful, industrial, manufacturing nation. As she says, 'My story is the story of Great Britain, / The United Kingdom, The British Empire' (p. 73).

In Scene 15, Lamplighter tells of her resolve to write down her story and pass it on. Despite all efforts to prevent it from being published, she succeeded. In chorus with the other women, she proclaims the Bill to abolish the slave trade put forward in the House of Commons in 1792 but condemns the fact that the Bill was not passed. Slave rebellions broke out on many of the islands of the West Indies and, in 1804, St Dominique achieved 'the only completely successful slave rebellion in world history and becomes the Republic of Haiti' (p. 79). The threat of the Napoleonic War to British political power, its West Indian colonies and the Atlantic trade was a catalyst for the passing of the Bill to Abolish the Slave Trade in 1807, but the trade continued. Lamplighter comments 'More slave ships sailed the shark filled sea' (p. 80), and it was not until 1838 that the Bill to abolish slavery, the institution itself, passed its second reading in the House of Commons on condition that slave owners should be generously compensated. At the end of this scene Lamplighter reports that in August 1838 the Baptist Church in Falmouth, Jamaica was decorated with flowers and a coffin was inscribed with the words 'Colonial slavery died July 31 1838' (p. 83).

In the final scene, entitled 'Freedom', Lamplighter reiterates that 'One day I finally managed to tell / My story' (p. 84) and have it printed and reprinted. She states that, in the act of remembering, the years had caught up with her and she is able to see herself again as the young girl, Anniwaa in her African village, 'Her hair plaited with thread [...] wearing her mother's yellow head-tie' (p. 85) and only then could she begin to tell her story. She speaks as Anniwaa voicing

once more her terrible fear in the darkness of the dungeon
of Cape Coast Castle. The play ends with the words she spoke
at the opening: 'Once upon a time, I lived in a house with a
cone-shaped roof, in a big compound. My mother grew okra
and pumpkin in her yard. My father shaped wood and metal.'
(p. 87).

2. Black Harriot

In Scene 6, Black Harriot tells us that she had been bought
on the Guinea Coast, taken to St Kitts in the West Indies
and sold to 'Big Fat Planter' (p. 18), a plantation owner who
fathered two of her children when she was still a young
girl. The plantation owner brought her and her children to
England. He subsequently died of smallpox, leaving her penni-
less. She tells us that she became a prostitute in order to
survive, teaching herself to read in the hope, as she wryly
comments, that 'a polite whore would fare better in the streets
of London' (p. 19). She describes the degrading treatment
she was subjected to in order to ensure she fetched the best
price in the slave market:

> When I arrived off the ship
> I was polished with palm oil
> To make my dusky skin shine.
> My anus was plugged with wadding.   (p. 24)

She was given a new name, Harriot, and, since there was once
a White Harriot, she explains, she was known as Black Harriot.
In common with the other women slaves, she was repeatedly
subjected to sexual assault by her owner. She resisted, fighting
back against the rapists.

   In Scene 8, Black Harriot refers to the sugar trade which
had made the plantation owners and traders rich: 'My story
is the story of sugar. / I was stolen for sugar' (p. 41). In the

following scene, she describes the horrific deaths of men, women and children on the slave ships. A ship's captain, Luke Collingwood, had chosen to throw living slaves into the sea in order to claim insurance on each life. Black Harriot speaks of those who, in a last desperate act of defiance, chose to throw themselves overboard:

> They dived down into the sea.
> Those were the deaths with wings,
> Like songs, like freedom songs,
> Rising up and out at last.
> No more, no more, no more, no more.   (p. 47)

She witnessed the deaths of women in the cane fields from deadly diseases and honours them by remembering their names, their ages and where they had originally come from. In Scene 11, she recounts the fates of women who ran away: 'Running away was a leap in the dark. / Running away was a search for the heart' (p. 55).

In Scene 13, the women recount and comment on the rapid growth of British cities made prosperous by the trade in sugar, tobacco and cotton. With pointed irony, Black Harriot, in a parody of the popular song 'Glasgow Belongs to Me', changes the word 'chap' in the line 'I'm only a common old working chap' (p. 65) to 'slave', condemning, with bleak humour, the greed for goods and profit, the rapacious capitalism which drove the industrial revolution and made Britain a powerful trading and political empire. She does not spare the role of Scotland in the slave trade, citing the many slaves, whose fathers were Scottish plantation owners in the West Indies, given Scottish names and in particular the role of the city of Glasgow which profited greatly from the slave trade. She states: 'My daughters have Scottish blood. / Scotland has my blood' (p. 73).

She remembers the slave risings in the islands of the West
Indies and speaks of 'A tinder spark from one small island'
(p. 81) lighting fires of rebellion in other islands. In the
closing scene, her words reflect her courage, resourcefulness
and resilience. She does not know what has become of her
children; she never knew her mother, but she endured. There
is a spirited assertion of the fact that she has survived against
all the odds: 'And I managed. Life's tough!' (p. 84). And her
final words have a defiance and humour which had helped to
sustain her throughout her life as a slave: 'This sure as hell
is my story!' (p. 87).

3. Constance

In Scene 6, Constance tells us that she was given her new name
so that she 'would be a virtue [...] To always be Constant –
reliable, / Sturdy, neger wench' (p. 26). Transported to St
Lucia, she laboured at first in the cane fields then was put to
work in the plantation owner's house. She found that the
'HouseLady' was just as demanding as any field driver. She
gave the HouseLady's children the care they lacked from
their mother. Constance states:

> Her children talk my talk
> And walk my walk
> And know me better than their mother.
> The children know my songs.   (p. 29)

There is a bitter irony in the fact that a slave woman, seen as
a chattel or a beast of burden by the so-called civilised races,
so often gave her master's children the nurture and love that
their parents neglected to give.

Like Black Harriot, Constance was sexually assaulted and
exploited by the plantation owner and his friends. We learn
that her daughter had been taken from her and she imagines

that one day she would find her. She describes her hope as a lamp 'glowing deeply' inside her which cannot be extinguished (p. 34). In Scene 8, Constance continues her story, telling us that the slave traders had taken her three-year-old girl to be sold. When she was pregnant, she had wished she could have made her daughter look ugly in order to prevent her from being sexually exploited when she had grown into a young girl of 'nine ten eleven' (p. 41). We also learn that her other three children had been taken from her. Traumatised, she had lost her speech for many months. She recounts the taking of her daughter, describing their last walk hand in hand to the 'Big House'. She will never forget 'the feeling of a small child's hand' in hers (p. 45). Constance's tragedy is that she was robbed of her child, brutally prevented from being her guide and support as she was growing up. In Scene 10, she continues her account of the taking of her three-year-old 'bean girl' (p. 51). She knows that, if they both run, they will be killed. She admits that she had thought of suffocating her daughter rather than have her suffer a living death in slavery. It is only the small lamp of hope that her daughter will be found which prevents her.

Towards the end of Scene 13, in which the women catalogue and comment on the historical facts of the cities' exponential growth, Constance reminds us, in virtually the same words as Lamplighter had used, that she had put the city of Glasgow on the map. At the end of the scene, she reveals that she had been brought as a child to Barbados by the Royal Africa Company.

In the final scene of the play, Constance recounts that eventually she got her freedom. She had to work to buy her shack and pay back the owners. She became a grandmother to all the neighbourhood children. Her final words speak poignantly of the shocking cruelty of the slave trade which robbed children of their childhood, of their mother's care and love and treated them as chattels to be used and abused as they grew up. She says: 'One day I would like to tell my grandchildren. / If I could find them; I would tell them' (p. 87).

4. Mary

Mary tells us in Scene 6 that she had been a field hand on a sugar plantation. Subjected to back-breaking labour, she and her fellow slaves had hacked out fields from a 'frontier wilderness' (p. 19). She had moved from third gang to first gang (suggesting that she was prized as a hard and skilled worker), planting, cutting and loading the sugar cane from youth to old age. She worked quickly, singing, as she says, 'to stop me dying in the sugar cane' (p. 20). She miscarried and could not have any further children. She compares her wrinkled hands to 'the roots of old trees'. Like the other women she was raped repeatedly by her master, silently enduring the assaults until she finally retaliated, hitting him across the back of his head. Her punishment was extreme. She recounts that she was flogged, then tied to a tree and left for dead for three days as an example to other slaves who dared to fight back. She survived the crucifixion but was scarred for life. Her only comfort was in her Christian faith. As she says:

> I knew I had been born again
> And that the Lord Christ himself
> Had come to give me salvation.   (p. 23)

Brought to Jamaica as a young girl in 1792, she was given the name Mary McDonald. During the Jamaican slave rising, she did not have the physical strength to run away but found comfort in her faith. In the closing scene of the play, Mary tells us that she found a free man who loved her despite her scarred body. He had tried to buy her freedom but her owner would not let her go. Eventually her owner, his wife and the overseer died, leaving Mary a free woman. Against the most terrible odds she had survived. Her final words remind us that the story of her suffering, in common with the testimonies of Lamplighter, Black Harriot and Constance, is a true one: 'This happened to me, the Lord knows it's the truth' (p. 87).

Language and Style
Jackie Kay gives the four women the full range of linguistic expression emphasising their intelligence, sensitivity and spirit: the very humanity they were denied by their individual masters and the institution of slavery, which treated them as chattels to be exploited and abused. In bearing witness to their own suffering and the suffering of others, they claim and assert the rights due to all humankind.

The women's stories are told in prose and poetry, their testimonies an interweaving of everyday colloquial speech, the more formal register of the telling of their stories, the registers of legal and historical documents, dramatic monologue, poetic lament and song. They employ vivid imagery, irony, repetition and fugue-like sequences throughout the play. The following examples will illustrate the verbal density of the text and its linguistic variety.

1. Scenes 1 and 2 (pp. 1–4)

In Scene 1, Lamplighter, as her younger self Anniwaa, gives voice to her thoughts and feelings as she waits, incarcerated in the dungeon of Cape Coast Castle to be taken on board a slave ship. She begins in the present tense: 'I am a girl. I am in the dark [...] I don't know where I am', then uses the storyteller's device to tell us her past story: 'Once upon a time, I lived in a house with a cone-shaped roof, in a big compound'. She speaks as a young girl in mainly short sentences with few complex or compound clauses. Returning to the present tense, she tells us of her kidnapping by slavers, the beatings and abuse she is subjected to on the journey to the fort on the West African coast. There she is separated from her brother and imprisoned in the dungeon of the fort. She describes her terror vividly. 'Kept like an animal' she hears a sound she has never heard before: 'They say it is The Sea. I think it is a wild monster. I think it is coming for me' (p. 2).

In this opening scene, the poet/dramatist has created an individual who, in giving voice to her suffering, enables us to imagine how slavery affected a person's whole physical and psychological being.

In Scene 2, entitled 'Shipping News' (pp. 3–4), the four women – Lamplighter (as Anniwaa in maturity), Black Harriot, Constance and Mary – and the one male character, MacBean, are introduced. MacBean speaks in the language of a weather report and of a Captain's log:

Wednesday 29 May –
Buryed a Boy slave, No 86 of a flux.
Decreasing. Rough or very rough.   (p. 4)

The women speak in turn, commenting on the inhumanity of the captain who does not name individual slaves, referring to them only as numbers. They comment on the ferocious weather of the Atlantic passage. Constance, in using the metaphor 'The moon was in a shroud' (p. 3), is perhaps commenting on the weather conditions when the moon was part obscured by mist or faintly shining through the 'shrouds' part of the rigging of the ship. Her allusion is bleakly apt for there were no shrouds, winding sheets, for the slaves who were hurriedly committed to the sea. Black Harriot's poetic monologue is a lament for them and conveys the utter desolation and violence of the 'howling, moaning Atlantic' as 'another body yet' is thrown 'Into the open-grave-green sea'. At the end of the scene, Mary makes the bitterly ironic comment: 'If you want to learn to pray, / Go to sea.'

2. Scene 6 (pp. 16–35)

In this key scene the women tell their stories, testifying to the power of memory which sustains them in the hardest of times. Their monologues alternate with fugue-like sequences where a fragment of a theme is voiced by each woman in turn to be followed by further thematic fragments, all contributing to the exposition of the women's experiences as commodities in the slave markets, as field hands in the sugar plantations and as servants in the plantation owners' houses.

The scene begins with Lamplighter's monologue where she creates a picture of her childhood world before she was kidnapped and sold into slavery. In blank verse she describes her life in her West African village where she played with her brother and friends, admired her father's skill in shaping wood and metal, visited the snake spirit and felt secure in her house with its cone-shaped roof. Most of all she remembers that she and her brother belonged to the whole village. The repetition of the phrase 'I remember' reinforces the emotional intensity of her act of remembering 'the life before'. It seems to her that it was another girl who had 'lived that blessed life': a 'mysterious magical girl' who had 'climbed to the top of trees' (p. 16) and had never seen the sea. Her words are lyrical and elegiac in stark contrast to her account of the brutality and horror of the Atlantic passage:

> What I tell is not a story:
> How they hid me in a sack,
> [...]
> How I smelt the blood on the galley.
> How I heard the cries of women and children.   (p. 28)

Black Harriot's monologues are shorter and more colloquial.
She is forthright and deploys humour:

> Nobody told my story before.
> You better listen good, girl.
> Or I'm going to tell it twice!   (p. 17)

There is a wry humour in her explanation of the name she
was given by her master and a forthright mockery of the men
who exploited her sexually. Her account of her enslavement
is matter of fact: 'I was taken to St Kitts and sold / To Big
Fat Planter' and there is a natural justice in her refusal to
use her master's actual name. Her words reveal a defiant
spirit which will not be intimidated despite the brutality of
her treatment.

Constance is a quieter, more stoical personality. She speaks
less colloquially than Black Harriot. Stating the fact that
she was forced to be subservient always to her master and
mistress, she expresses with quiet anger that she was named
Constance 'So that in my abstraction / I would forever be
constant' (p. 25). In a series of parallel phrases, she conveys
her anger:

> At the side of, but not seen by,
> In the house of, but not heard by,
> In the bed of, but not loved by,
> [...]

Her words build to a bitter climax: 'To always be Constant –
reliable, / Sturdy, neger wench!' (p. 26).

The latter phrase, echoing the words used by the merchants
in the slave markets to promote a sale, is spoken by Constance
with justified contempt. She is very aware of the role assigned

to her by her master and mistress and fulfils it faithfully looking after her mistress's children with loving care. She expresses her feelings for them eloquently:

> Her children talk my talk
> And walk my walk
> And know me better than their mother.
> These children know my songs   (p. 29)

The words of songs are part of her discourse. She plays on the words of 'Rub a dub / Three men in a tub' in an ironic comment on the constant cleaning and polishing she is required to do. In this scene, she sings a Creole lullaby and joins in singing with the other women. At the end of the scene, she speaks poignantly of her constant hope that one day she would see her children again.

Mary evokes her life as a field hand in the sugar plantations, working with speed and efficiency, 'singing', as she says without exaggeration, 'to stop me dying in the sugar cane'. A field hand all her days, she tells of the toll it has taken on her body, describing her wrinkled hands with fingers 'like bindweed, / Knarled and crossed over themselves, / Like the roots of old trees'. The imagery she uses emphasises the harshness of the working conditions she endured throughout her life. She describes the rapes she suffered at the hands of her master, remaining 'silent as the moon' until she finally retaliated: 'I hit him and hit him again'. Her punishment was extreme. She was flogged then tied to a tree and left for dead. Having survived this crucifixion she feels she has been born again: 'that the Lord Christ himself / Had come to give me salvation'. Her words echo the biblical teaching of her master and mistress who teach their slaves Christian precepts but do not practise them. Her Christian belief in salvation,

however, sustains her and gives her hope despite the extreme
hardships she endured.

3. Scene 13 (pp. 62–74)

In this scene Jackie Kay uses fugue-like sequences, reitera-
tions of the key theme of the exponential growth and prosperity of many British cities due to the slave trade. The women
condemn the greed and exploitation, reiterating in turn the
names of the cities which had profited, the commodities manu-
factured, the banks and prestigious buildings erected and the
fortunes made. Their declamations dramatically highlight
this economic boom:

> ALL   Boom! Boom! Boom!
> CONSTANCE   Liverpool, Bristol, London, Manchester,
>   Lancaster, Glasgow
> BLACK HARRIOT   Brass!
> LAMPLIGHTER   Glassware!
> MARY   Banking!   (p. 62)

The women make verbal play of the noun and suffix 'ship' in
a fugue-like sequence: 'Ship bread, ship biscuit, ship breaker,
slaver, ship broker, [...] ship rat, slaver, ship days'. Every
fourth word in Constance's declaration is 'slaver', emphasising
the interconnectedness of the slave trade system. The theme
is further developed by MacBean and Constance who explore
the various meanings of 'ship' as a verb and a suffix. Constance
brings the sequence to a climax with her repetition of the word
'AuthorSHIP'.

  In the course of this scene the women sing in protest:

> *But the banks are made of marble*
> *With a guard at every door*
> *And the vaults are stuffed with silver*
> *That the people sweated for.*

They parody popular songs such as 'I Belong to Glasgow' and 'Money Makes the World Go Round' and voice the excited shouts of speculators: 'Share prices going up! Up up! Invest now!' MacBean adopts the role of chronicler quoting from the rhetoric of an anti-abolitionist's speech – 'Fellow citizens of Bristol. Do not lay the axe at the root of your own prosperity by supporting the abolition of slavery!' (p. 67) – and from historical accounts: 'Bishop Pococke visited Glasgow in 1760. He remarked, "this city has above all others felt the advantages of the union in the West Indian trade"' (p. 66). This use of intertextual references highlights how embedded the slave trade was in the whole fabric of Britain as a rapidly expanding trading and industrial empire. By reiterating this theme throughout Scene 13, the women emphasise Britain's complicity in this brutal system.

4. Scene 15 (pp. 76–83)

In this scene, MacBean recounts that thirteen thousand residents of Glasgow in 1792 put their names to a petition to abolish slavery to be presented to the House of Commons. The women in turn give their responses to this statement:

> CONSTANCE Condemnation
> MACBEAN that its sentence is sealed;
> MARY Sealed!
> MACBEAN that this curse of mankind is seen by the House
> in its true light;
> LAMPLIGHTER true light (p. 77)

Again in choral reiteration, the women list the rebellions which arose on the many West Indian islands. They declaim: 'Immediate, not gradual abolition!' (p. 78). Their declamations chart the slow progress towards abolition, citing further risings in the West Indies which led to brutal punishments for insurrection. Their words come to a climax in MacBean's statement, quoting the historical account: 'On Friday, July 26, 1833, the Bill for the Abolition of Slavery passes its second reading in the House of Commons after an agreement is reached to generously compensate the slave owners' (p. 82). In the most telling of the intertextual references, MacBean quotes the words engraved on the Abolitionist Society's medal: 'Am I not a Man and a Brother?'. This rhetorical question is modified by Lamplighter, Constance and Mary who ask in turn: 'Am I not a Woman and a Sister?' (p. 81). At the end of the scene the women sing the spiritual: '*I went down in the valley one day / Good Lord, show me the way*' (p. 83), expressing the hope for freedom which had never been extinguished.

Lamplighter has the last word, citing the symbolic burying of a coffin filled with chains, collars and whips in the Baptist Church in Falmouth, Jamaica. The coffin was inscribed with the historic words: 'Colonial Slavery died July 31 1838'.

Through detailed historical research and by combining her skills as a poet and dramatist, Jackie Kay has created in *The Lamplighter* a powerful work of the creative imagination. Above all it is a haunting and lasting memorial to the count-less women, men and children sold into slavery.

iii. Persecution and Isolation

'**Whilst Leila Sleeps**' (*Darling*, p. 65) is a dramatic monologue which portrays the desperate situation of a mother and her child apprehended by unknown authorities as they flee from their home. The use of first-person narrative brings us directly into the woman's experience. She may be a refugee fleeing from war or a citizen arrested by the agents of a totalitarian regime. There is an absence of a specific context which gives the speaker's situation a universal relevance, reinforcing the reality of the exercise of arbitrary power visited upon citizens in many regimes.

The title of the poem suggests a lullaby, a cradle song, but that expectation is abruptly cancelled in the first line which raises the question: why is the speaker 'moving in the dead of night'? This phrase expresses the speaker's urgent need to leave undetected and suggests the threat of impending danger. The speaker, whom it can be assumed is a woman, wishes to be in her mother's house, the implication being that it is a place of safety, but her mother is far away on the other side of the world. Her words convey vulnerability. We learn that she is alone with her child, Leila, who is described as 'a bundle in her car seat'. Leila is sleeping peacefully but her mother fears that it is 'the sleep of oblivion', that the sleep of death may come.

The tense, threatening atmosphere is heightened by the personification of the headlights of the car as 'paranoic eyes / sweeping the streets for – what?'. The question 'for what?' emphasises the mother's sense of a danger she is unable to identify. It also suggests she is questioning whether she is over-reacting to her fears, allowing her imagination to over-rule her rational self. And for a split second she thinks she is safe 'before they appeared'. The sense of menace deepens as her unidentified pursuers, described as 'the men in plain suits', ask her name and take her driving license and identity papers. Their smiles are sinister, heightening her fears. We must ask the questions: Who are they? Why are they following her? Why do they want her name? Why are they taking her papers from her? Alone, she has no-one to bear witness to their inquisition. She has no choice: she must go with 'the men in the plain suits' who are not recognisable as police officers or soldiers.

When Leila wakens, she tries to reassure her with soothing words but her voice is hollow. She feels exposed and bereft of

all security, expressing her desperation in the violent metaphor 'My voice is a house with the roof / blown off'. The final
verse begins with the stark statement 'We are done for'.
She can see no escape from this situation and cannot hide
her predicament from her daughter. Her words, 'The night
dreams / my terror', suggest that the darkness of the night
and the tailing of her car heighten her terror to hallucinatory
levels. Despite her terror, she responds with a gesture of love
to her child, who is tugging at her coat, by whispering a lullaby,
Leila's 'cradle song'. In need of comfort and reassurance, the
child holds on to her mother as they are taken away to an
unknown destination and an unknown fate.

Gastarbeiter is the German term for a foreign migrant
worker, literally a guest worker. After the Second World War,
there was a shortage of labour in Northern European countries and high unemployment in Southern European countries.
In order to rebuild its economy, Germany instituted a formal
guest worker scheme from 1955 until 1973. The original
plan was for temporary residence but after a number of
years many guest workers qualified for permanent residence.
Many Northern European countries adopted similar schemes.
Migrant workers were and continue to be victims of prejudice
and to be targeted by far-right organisations in many European
countries.

The poem entitled **'Gastarbeiter'** (*Darling*, pp. 81–82)
portrays the circumstances of a guest worker and her fears
for the safety of her children and extended family. In verse
one, the poet evokes the mother's sense of disorientation when
she first came to the new country. There is no indication of
where she had come from but her new environment is alien to
her. The expressions 'the trees were tall strangers' and 'the
air was diesel' suggest that she had come from a rural environment, perhaps desert or semi-desert, to work in a busy town
or city. Although she had learned the language of her new

country, she spoke hesitantly 'like a faltering step', this simile and the repetition of the adjective 'quick' emphasising her nervousness and lack of confidence as she walks to work in busy streets. Her instinct is to be self-effacing. We learn that she is a seamstress working in a factory, perhaps a sweatshop where low-paid workers are exploited. The reference to 'a sharp needle' suggests pain as she works the 'long swathes/of material, long enough to wrap / twice around the dead', the lengths of cloth suggesting burial shrouds. The onomatopoeic word 'jabbering' evokes the unpleasant repetitive sound of the sewing machine as she prepares to finish the garment by hand.

Her home is 'a narrow house', which suggests she lives in cramped conditions. Reading the fairy tale *Hansel and Gretel*, she learns new words and finds that elements of this unsettling tale resonate with her. Like Hansel and Gretel, she and her children have been propelled by poverty into a hostile environment and must develop resilience and strategies for survival. Her troubling dreams are personified as 'uninvited guests, / folding white wraps for small children', again suggesting the preparation of shrouds for the dead. The poet further develops the imagery of 'long swathes / of material' in the following verse, describing the mother and her children sharing a bed by the metaphor 'rolled / tight, a bandage on an open wound'. In straitened circumstances they sleep close together for comfort and security. She sleeps lightly and in her dreams the stars take on 'the shapes of swastikas'. She is aware of the terrible legacy of the Holocaust and in her nightmare gathers up her children in her arms and jumps from the burning house. The image of the grandmother, mother and daughter as 'ghosts in another room' emphasises the age-old irrational fear and suspicion of strangers which leads to the scapegoating of particular ethnic, social or family groups. The poem powerfully conveys the mother's vulnerability and fears for her own and her children's future.

5. IDENTITY AFFIRMED

i. Love and Friendship

The transformative power of love and friendship in their many forms is a theme embedded in Jackie Kay's poetry. Many of her poems celebrate enduring relationships of love and friendship but many others explore the pain, hurt and regret of troubled or failed relationships. She expresses these feelings with a frankness and generosity of spirit which seeks understanding rather than blame.

Kay wrote **'Pas de Deux'** (*Bantam*, pp. 24–26) in response to a commission by Scottish Ballet. It was subsequently made into a short film by Eve McConnachie called *Haud Close Tae Me*. In classical ballet, the *pas de deux* is a dance duet in which a male and female dance together. It is usually the climax of a love story. In modern dance it can be performed by dancers of the same sex but the principle remains the same: the portrayal of a courtship ritual and a celebration of sexual love. It is both a tribute to the skill and artistry of the dancers of Scottish Ballet and a verbal duet on the theme of love. It is in the form of a dialogue between lovers, one of whom seeks reassurance that their love will endure and the other affirms his/her love in a declaration of faithfulness. The verses of the poem echo the rhythms of the dance, suggesting its 'birling' movement and the repetition of the speaker's questions in his/her verses throughout the poem further reinforces the various stages of their conversation:

> Would you take haud o' me,
> > Take haud o' me
> Haud me in your airms an' birl me aroon?

The running motif of technical ballet terms for the steps of the dancers charts the stages of their conversation. The use of colloquial Scots brings a warmth and intimacy to their dialogue.

In their opening exchanges, the first speaker asks for an affirmation of their love expressing both hope for love and intimacy and an anxiety that he/she might be led astray. The second speaker replies with a declaration and a promise: 'I'll keep time wey you, / Bide close tae you'. The following verses chart the further stages of their conversation. The second speaker pledges to keep faith 'Until the moon draps tae the sea', perhaps echoing the lines of Robert Burns's love song 'My Love is Like a Red, Red Rose': 'I will luve thee still, my Dear, / Till a' the seas gang dry.' The last two verses bring their verbal duet to a climax with the declaration that they have become as one – 'You go; I'll follow / [...] Till I am you and you are me' – and a reiteration of the invitation to join together in dance and the acceptance of it. The use of the 'patter' associated with Glasgow dance halls in the heyday of ballroom dancing, 'Are you dancing?' and 'Are you asking?', gives the final exchange of the couple warmth and immediacy and unites the twin themes of the poem: a tribute to the formal skills and artistry of the ballet dancers and a celebration of love in all its anxious anticipation, exhilaration and joie de vivre. It celebrates the universal dance of love in its many cultural manifestations.

'Other Lovers' (*Darling*, pp. 94–96) is a six-poem monologue which charts a couple's relationship from the intense joy of being in love through the stages of its breakdown and finally to an emotional equilibrium found in the acceptance of their separation.

The first poem, 'What was it you said again there by the river', expresses the intense joy and exhilaration of being in love and a fleeting anxiety which seeks reassurance in the repeated question 'Do you love me?'. The poet likens the optimism of the young lovers 'who danced to an old song', making reference to a song by The Bee Gees, '*how deep do you feel?*', and perhaps the conceit of 'an old song' being a universal metaphor for the state of love. Kay uses cosmic imagery, 'the moon split in two / the stars smashed', to express love's ecstasy. She describes a walk by the river, a kiss in the dark and the sound of ducks on the river startling the silence of the night.

The second poem, entitled 'The Day You Change', describes the changes in behaviour and attitude which mark the breakdown in their relationship. Conversation is no longer natural or relaxed: the phrase 'you always say' becomes a sign of annoyance and the phrase 'pass the pepper' becomes a wry comment on the limited conversation of mealtimes. There is no longer the emotional comfort of a shared bed.

In the third poem, 'When you move out', the poet describes the speaker's realisation of the reality of separation. Her estranged lover packs her possessions, the speaker acknowledging that 'You won't miss things'. The paraphernalia of a shared life is not what matters; it is the sadness and regret that their life together, with all its various activities, is no longer possible. The poem ends on a sombre note: 'There's no point, // growing peonies to blossom without you', the speaker bluntly telling herself to 'take up something else'.

The fourth poem, entitled 'Swim', begins with the metaphor 'at the end of a perfect rainbow' to suggest their previous happy existence but it is immediately followed by the blunt phrase 'you have upped and left' and the bleakly ironic reference to her taking up swimming as a displacement activity. She comments with a wry humour: 'This is the way of love'. This poem in the sequence ends with the speaker admitting that she dwells obsessively on their previous physical intimacy.

The fifth poem, 'She never thought she could with anyone else', reveals that the speaker has a new lover, but, addressing her former lover, she asserts 'But you are always standing on her shoulders'. She sees in her new lover similarities with her former lover, some of which she finds irritating. She compares her new lover's making of a bed unfavourably with the 'smooth corners, no creases' of her former lover's bed-making. Her catalogue of her new lover's habits reveals her inner conflict, the sense of being in an emotional limbo.

The final poem, 'Worse than that', marks a further stage in the process of accepting and coming to terms with their separation. It begins with the dramatic line 'One day you find you are your other lover'. The speaker realises that she has unconsciously adopted many of the same mannerisms and attitudes characteristic of her former lover. This has an unsettling effect leading to the speaker becoming uncertain of herself and losing confidence: 'You are scared to go from A to B'. The metaphor 'she was the map-reader' reveals how much the speaker depended on her former lover. The penultimate section of this poem marks her gradual regaining of confidence: 'Out and about [...] / winding your way past yourself'. Humorously she recounts mastering the then new ATM device: 'Catch your slick tenners, *No bother*'. Her final words express her pleasure in her regained confidence: 'You have a whole new life.'

By using detailed description of the everyday actions and consequences arising from the lovers' separation, the speaker charts the emotional toll it has taken on her and the gradual acceptance without bitterness of the finality of their separation.

Written to mark her parents' sixtieth wedding anniversary, **'Diamond Colonsay'** (*Bantam*, pp. 9–10) is both celebratory and reflective. The poet addresses her parents, paying tribute to their enduring relationship which has enriched their lives and the poet's life.

It is written in four-line verses, many of which rhyme, enabling the poet to pay tribute to her parents in a form suited to a lyrical, reflective mood. The first verse expresses the poet's joy as she sees her parents 'come down the stairs at Glassard' on the morning of their sixtieth anniversary. Their visit to Colonsay is described as like 'a surprise honeymoon'. The beauty of the island of Colonsay becomes synonymous with the enduring beauty of her parents' love for each other. Kay describes the timeless landscape of the island in alliterative phrases: 'the shimmering sea' and the 'seals slither off rocks to the bay'. In her description of her parents' singing to one another every day, there is perhaps the suggestion of an affinity with seal songs, of being in tune with the natural world. Her parents' singing is also natural and unforced. She pays tribute to their companionship: they are 'Comrades, compadres, companions'. She describes their walking and the climbing of Scotland's mountains over the years in lyrical terms: it is an expression of 'Love on the rise of the lapwing's wing'. They sing as they walk past the golden sands of Kiloran Bay to a circle of standing stones, iconic features of the landscape of the Western Isles. The more formal lyrical description is punctuated by more colloquial expressions describing everyday experiences in their lives: 'Sixty years of ding-dong' and the time found 'in the kitchen for a wee dance'.

The poem ends with a toast to her spirited, life-affirming parents: 'Call it Colonsay, the call of Colonsay! / Helen and John, John and Helen Kay.' With a modulation of tone from the celebratory to the reflective, punctuated by more informal comment, the poem is brought to a climax with a toast to her remarkable parents. It captures precious family experiences and shares them with us.

Jackie Kay has called **'Brendon Gallacher'** (*Darling*, p. 201) an ode to childhood. It touchingly recreates the voice of her younger self recounting the story of her friendship with her imagined friend, Brendon Gallacher. Her account emphasises the importance of this imaginary friend to her and demonstrates the power of her imagination. She gives him a very different family background from her own. The first verse expresses the differences between them in a series of contrasts: his father was a cat burglar; her father was a full-time worker for the Communist party. He had six brothers; she had one.

She tells us that Brendon, despite that background, had noble aspirations, to take his mother for 'A wee holiday some place nice'. But when her mother suggests that she invites him round for dinner, the poet invents a number of excuses to avoid being found out. The crunch comes when, two years later, her mother discovers that there is no Brendon Gallacher. The intrusion of reality has a dramatic effect on the young girl. The final verse seems to blend her emotional reactions as a young girl with her own adult recollections of the hold that her imaginary friend had on her imagination. Dramatically she gives voice to the sudden realisation that her imaginings have been found out and that she could no longer pretend that he was real. The last three lines reflect the vivid picture she still has of him with 'his spiky hair, / his impish grin, his funny flapping ear' and emphasise the emotional importance to her of this imaginary companion who continues to live so vividly in her mind.

'**Darling**' (*Darling*, p. 228) is a poem of great tenderness which expresses the poet's feelings about a loved one who has died. The poet does not reveal the person's identity or circumstances but there is the suggestion that the person knew she was dying as she wept 'curled into the shape of a half moon', and perhaps an allusion to the effects of ageing on the body's frame in the phrase 'smaller than herself' as she lies in the foetal position. By using the second person rather than the first person and repeating the phrase 'You might forget' in the first verse, the poet addresses not just herself but includes the reader or listener in her particular experience, voicing her fear that she might not remember the sound of her loved one's voice or her face when asleep. Using enjambment, the poet leads us into the second verse in which she states the apparent paradox: 'she seemed already to be leaving / before she left'. The contrast between the inevitability of death and the renewal of spring is poignant. The poet speaks now in the first person, stating simply and directly that she had held her loved one's hand and had sung to her as she passed away peacefully, imagining her as 'a slip of a girl again' free from care and suffering. She had sung 'The Mingulay Boat Song' to her, a song learned by generations of primary school children. It is a song in which the sailors of Mingulay in the Outer Hebrides sing of sailing home to their families and in a sense the poet is using the song as a metaphor for death: '*let her go boys*'. She imagines her 'skipping off, / her heart light, her face almost smiling'.

The final verse alludes to the complex feelings which the poet could not recognise or express in the immediate aftermath of death, then concludes with a strong inclusive affirmation that the dead live on in our memories, not in a morbid sense but in the sense of our finding solace in the precious memories we hold of those we have loved. They are still present, 'holding our hands', a continuing source of comfort and support. The poem has an unpretentious dignity which expresses poignantly the deep feelings the poet had for her friend.

6. CONCLUSION

For Jackie Kay, the need to connect, include and bear witness is essential to her role as a writer and cultural ambassador. Her work captures the complexities of life with warmth, wit and a keen sympathetic eye for human frailty. She has a sharp ear for individuals' speech patterns and a love of song. Her poems, expressing an individual's experience of racism, slavery and persecution, are a searing indictment of humankind's inhumanity. Her poetry speaks to us and for us all.

7. BIBLIOGRAPHY

Fiction

> *Trumpet* (Picador, published 1998, republished 2011)
> *Why Don't You Stop Talking* (Picador, 2002)
> *Wish I Was Here* (Picador, 2006)
> *Reality Reality* (Picador, 2011)

Non-Fiction

> Biography: *Bessie Smith* (Absolute Press, 1997; Faber and Faber Ltd, 2021)
> Memoir: *Red Dust Road: An Autobiographical Journey* (Picador, published 2010, republished 2017)

Poetry

> *Other Lovers* (Bloodaxe Books Ltd, 1993)
> *Two's Company* (Puffin, 1994)
> *Three Has Gone* (Puffin, 1994)
> *Off Colour* (Bloodaxe Books Ltd, 1998)
> *The Frog Who Dreamed She Was an Opera Singer* (Bloomsbury Children's Books, 1998)
> *Life Mask* (Bloodaxe Books Ltd, 2005)
> *Darling: New & Selected Poems* (Bloodaxe Books Ltd 2007, republished 2016)
> *Red Cherry Red* (Bloomsbury Children's Books, 2007)
> *Fiere* (Picador, 2011)
> *The Empathetic Store* (Mariscat Press, 2015)
> *Bantam (*Picador, 2017)

Poetic Drama

> *Chiaroscuro* (Methuen Publishing Ltd, 1986; Oberon, 2019)
> *The Adoption Papers* (Bloodaxe Books Ltd, 1991, republished 2018)

Strawgirl (Macmillan Children's Books, 2002)
The Lamplighter (Bloodaxe Books Ltd, 2008; Picador, republished 2020)

Review

Morna Fleming, '*The Lamplighter*', in *ScotLit* 40 (Association for Scottish Literature, 2010)

Conference Paper

Dorothy McMillan, 'The Poetry of Carol Ann Duffy and Jackie Kay', Association for Scottish Literature Annual Schools Conference 2013 (ASL website and YouTube)

Interviews

Nick Major, 'The SRB Interview: Jackie Kay', in *Scottish Review of Books* 11.3 (2016)
Peter Ross, 'Interview: Jackie Kay on putting her adoption on stage', *Guardian*, 17 August 2019

Milton Keynes UK
Ingram Content Group UK Ltd.
UKHW022240240823
427342UK00007B/132